SUCCESSFUL
TEAM
BUILDING

SUCCESSFUL TEAM BUILDING

How to Create Teams that Really Work

John Davis, Peter Millburn
Terry Murphy, Martin Woodhouse

**KOGAN
PAGE**

First published in 1992

Kogan Page Limited
120 Pentonville Road
London N1 9JN

British Library Cataloguing in Publication Data

A CIP record for this book is available from the British Library

ISBN 0 7494 0811 1

Typeset by Saxon Printing Ltd, Derby
Printed and bound in Great Britain by Biddles Ltd., Guildford and Kings Lynn.

Contents

Introduction

You're reading this, so you think teams are A Good Thing. So does almost everybody else. To most people, the team is something everyone should wish to join and only eccentric individualists express dissatisfaction with team working. Of course, we all accept that some teams may get it wrong, but building teams and fostering team spirit are considered a good thing.

The very word *team* is often applied as a blanket term for any group, division, department or section of an organisation. It doesn't matter how large or small the team, it is assumed that calling it a team will make it one. Teams often seem to be considered as the leader's property – so and so's team – with the faceless mass following behind. Most teams are assembled as if people were cogs to be fitted to a machine, usually by combining a number of function types: one manager, two clerks, one engineer etc.

Yet, without teams, the amount that can be accomplished in this world is very small. They are certainly vital to our modern industrialised life. A good team is a pleasure to work in. Members are more productive, their contribution is recognised and they feel valued for the work they have done.

When we started the work on TEAMBuilder, distilling the ten years of paper based development experience which preceded it, we had the simple objective of creating a computer assisted team development programme. However, as we progressed, we found that we had created something which continually grew in significance as people responded to the core concept: a *team of equals*. There were three key elements:

- Timing – management styles and work force expectations have been moving away from the multi-level hierarchy of command

and control management, towards a close working relation-
ship in a radically compressed structure.

■ Approach – the concept of a team of equals was engineered –
not just based on academic theory. The approach used was to
analyse successful teams and to find out what they were doing
to be successful.

■ Culture – the concept of a team of equals by its very nature
leads toward an open and supportive culture. This is the key to
both greater productivity and reduced stress.

All teams are put together with the best of intentions, yet not all
teams are successful teams. *Successful Team Building* will show you
how to turn your good intentions into a good team performance.
    So, **let's put a team on it!**

1

A Real Team

Everyone knows what a team is. Everyone knows how you put a team together. Everyone selects the best available team. Everyone knows how to pass out the tasks to be done among the team members. But if it's all so obvious, why do some teams succeed where others fail?

The team comes together in an endeavour to produce a level of performance greater than that which can be produced by individuals working alone. The whole should be greater than the sum of its parts. Yet in some cases the team just seems unable to work well together and produces less than a talented individual working alone.

The first proviso is that the team must be a real team. It must have a goal. It needs a reason to exist and for the team to work together, otherwise it will end up as a self-perpetuating body which exists to hold meetings – or in other words, a committee. Only when the team's purpose in existing has been established, can we start to put it together successfully. But what sort of team do we have in mind? There are so many types to choose from.

A group of followers

'Give me some people who can take orders and carry them out.' The authoritarian approach to team leadership was held in high regard in the hire and fire days of largely unskilled or semi-skilled work forces. It may seem feudalistic today, but it lurks beneath the surface of many a newly promoted team leader.

'Let's play follow the leader...' 'Me first, me first!' If the child is the father of the man, mental conditioning to want to lead starts early. Political leader, great general, or just the person at the top, the glory of charismatic leadership is desired by most of us – even if it's only the occasional fantasy!

Not surprisingly, when we get the chance to lead a team, we usually think we are doing a fairly good job – after all the team should end up doing it our way! Yet, a recent survey showed that 60 per cent of subordinates considered their boss incompetent and 30 per cent thought them only adequate.

You and I, of course, are one of the privileged 10 per cent who are respected by all, but, for all the others, what goes wrong?

We often select people for leadership. We train them to be leaders. But we don't select and train people to be followers. Many attempts have been made to create groups of followers, ranging from harsh school systems which taught conformity and respect for authority, to full military training for all male members of the population who could not somehow evade it. Discipline was imposed by the hierarchy and directed towards the unquestioning following of orders, backed by sanctions which ranged from the stupid to the sadistic. It reinforced the 'them and us' feelings that coloured the attitudes of those expected to follow the orders. There are those that believe this resulted in a workforce trained as highly skilled skivers and barrack room lawyers, having spent their creative energies on learning to beat the system and avoid work during those critical formative years. So it doesn't look as though this is really a desirable way to train team members.

What if everyone is trained to lead, so that they understand the problems? Even if this was affordable, it is bound to crash. Apart from assuming that everyone wants to be a leader, this is a recipe for conflict: the young stags will always try out their leadership strength on the group. Sadly, instead of working in harmony together, a team of leaders always suppresses weaker members to the follower positions.

By all means go off and play boy scouts on an outward bound style leadership course if you think you will enjoy that sort of thing. It can be very refreshing, away from the day-to-day balancing of priorities and personalities. It may build your personal confidence as you cope with unfamiliar problems in a totally different environment. But don't kid yourself that this has much relevance to sustained and creative team working. You may find that your appointed followers just don't want to play it your way. How will you get them working with you if they won't willingly work for you? Treating all concerned as equals is a good beginning.

The BigTeam

This is the one big happy family concept, generated by the paternalistic view taken of those below by many top people. They mean well, but simply saying: 'We're all in this together, just one big team' does not make it so.

The term is applied to many groups who will never be a real team because they are too large to interact effectively. The desire to call a group a team is widespread, notably among function leaders and directors. We call it the BigTeam syndrome. This exhibits two common misconceptions about teamwork. First, it treats all the reporting staff as the personal property of the person at the top of the heap. They speak of them as 'my people'. As they are 'my people', they must be good. So it follows that they must be a team, because teams are a good thing. This applies the team label indiscriminately and devalues the association underlying real team working.

Secondly, to interact effectively as a team means that the numbers must be small enough to get together and let everyone contribute. The trouble is, once the numbers in the BigTeam get into double figures, communication and motivation become the real problems. Someone always gets missed out in the planning and decision making, therefore motivation becomes a problem because they don't feel fully involved or valued. Just getting the team together becomes a major exercise – you may not be able physically to get them all into one room for any other purpose than talking to them.

Teamwork depends on close working relationships and understanding. In our experience, a real team is simply not sustainable in a group of more than ten people – communication losses will ensure that it fragments into workable sub-groups (which may turn out to be the real teams).

The other problem with BigTeam thinking is that it is attractive to those who are primarily interested in personal power and influence. All too often it is the BigTeam leader who steamrollers the team into pursuing his personal agenda. This is only possible in a BigTeam situation, where the leader can adopt an isolated position by issuing orders through the chain of command and is yet another reason why the BigTeam is a suspect organism.

The real reason is that power players love BigTeams, because the BigTeam label is really about the acceptable face of office power politics. This is easily spotted when one BigTeam leader tries to score points off another BigTeam to further his or her ambitions.

The resulting internal wars can destroy individuals caught in the crossfire and even bleed organisations to death. Much BigTeam thinking has more in common with that of a military machine than with a real team.

The winning team

They must be a team, surely! Being part of the winning team is what our BigTeam friends are all about after all. So a successful football team, for example, must be a real team. There's a combination of functions for a start: striker, defender, goalkeeper.

But a sports team has only one purpose in life – to win. To this end the team members are simply replaceable components. The whole effort is directed towards producing a winning machine. Team members are trained to reproduce moves designed by people who are not even on the field of play – the set piece free kick is the most obvious example.

So it is only when you look behind the public face of the sports team at what is going on to make the team a success, that a true multidisciplinary team emerges: the builders of this team machine, the coaches, managers, physiotherapists, even the groundsmen, can be crucial to the winning team's performance.

The operating theatre team

To an outsider, this may appear to be the ultimate team fusion: surgeons, anaesthetist, nurses, all smoothly interlinking. A combination of skills all working together to achieve the noble end of healing. But imagine, if you will, a surgeon with eight arms who could hang from the ceiling – would he, she (or it) need a team? This team is another well oiled machine extending the reach, control and vision of the directing surgeon.

As such, these teams are only the executive function of a much larger team effort devoted to the total healing process. They represent yet another example of a single function team, which only has to work as a real team when tasks outside the function area have to be tackled. In cases like this, a core group, formed from those who consider themselves peers, tends to emerge as the real team.

The specialist team

Surely though, some specialist teams do exist. What about the sales team? They must have team spirit. They certainly seem to spend enough time talking about it!

Single function teams of this type can appear to show real team harmony. They should do – they are often very carefully made up of very similar people. To take a sales team as our example, they probably meet at regular intervals. One item that is always on the agenda at a sales meeting will be the sales figures for the team. There may even be a competition for best salesman. The key word here is *competition*. This is a team which is based on individualism rather than co-operation.

The specialist team represents a single discipline – sales, quality control, accounts. Its overall performance is rarely greater than the sum of its parts, because it is not about working together to achieve a common goal, but about individual efforts which have been combined for management and monitoring purposes only. It is only when this team faces a crisis and they need to lift their heads from the narrower day-to-day tasks, or to cope with managing change that they need to be a real team. As a result, the specialist team often needs help to respond successfully to a new challenge.

The project team

This by definition should be a multidisciplinary team, that relies on the effective combining of the assembled skills, knowledge and talents. It's often the first real team we attempt to put together in an organisation. Equally often, it starts out full of enthusiasm and then fails to produce on budget or on time. The best people were selected for the project, all the required specialist skills and knowledge were in place, yet something was missing.

How can it be that a team of highly qualified people can sit around a table, agree what has to be done, yet fail to complete vital tasks? Some teams seem to have a blind spot a mile wide:

- Team A keeps changing direction and fails to keep records;
- Team B spends too long planning and not enough time getting things done;
- Team C are over optimistic in their forecasting;
- Team D always seem to be working hard but get nowhere;
- Team E can identify but can't solve problems.

When the problems are pointed out, all these teams agree that they will do better next time and then end up in the same mess all over again. Good people with specialist skills are not always enough it seems. Chapter 5 will tell you why.

The Japanese model

The Japanese approach to teamworking has been held up as a model for everyone to marvel at and copy. Some companies attempting to achieve similar levels of success and productivity to Japanese competitors have latched on to this aspect of Japanese business life as if it were the only secret behind their commercial achievements.

It is apparently democratic. The trappings of the hierarchy – the separate manager's canteen, white collar v blue collar segregation – have been discarded. Single status is the order of the day. But, while the symbols of equality abound, the reality discloses a rigidly hierarchical structure. The Japanese have made it work in the cultures they create and manage in other countries by always taking the long view on investment and by targeting for high levels of performance in every area. However, they will tell you that their's is a very stressful culture.

The way this team functions is to place the team's needs above the personal goals of the individual. Personal aspirations are thus subjugated for the good of the team. It is a painstaking approach; all over the place little work groups gather together to input to the solution of problems and concentrate on the many details which contribute to quality and performance. It certainly seems to produce the goods and encourage contribution at every level, perhaps because they are prepared both to listen and to take many small steps to achieve a long-term goal.

Ours is an individualistic society. Even more so since the sixties and the cult of doing your own thing, reinforced by the changes and questioning attitudes of the Thatcher years. By harnessing the power and creativity of individuals, the British have shown that they can lead the world. The Nissan plant in the UK has outperformed its Japanese counterparts in many areas, apparently by harnessing more of this creative energy and releasing new ideas from within the workforce. Ideas that had always been suppressed until exposed to the Japanese team outlook.

How can creative self-expression, individual aspirations and teamwork be combined in harmony? How can we manage our businesses and teams with less dependence on a command and control hierarchy, which divides the world into 'them and us'?

The answer is to create the most productive team of all:

The team of equals

This team is not the easy option, but it is a fulfilling and satisfying place to work. In a team of equals you will see that:

■ Everyone pulls together, each contribution different yet valued.

■ Elements of leadership come from each member, appropriate to the needs of the team's activities at every stage. Adapting and developing as the capabilities and objectives change, they are willing to grow as a team and take on new challenges.

■ Goals are understood and accepted and they are not simply the vision of a single leader, however talented.

■ They are an effective group who can generate a sustained effort to achieve their team's objectives on time, on budget and to the highest possible quality.

■ Each member has enough confidence in his colleagues to pass on the leader's baton as the team progresses towards its objective, knowing that it will be passed back at the appropriate time. (They are never a leaderless team.)

For a team of equals, being the boss should mean that the others are encouraged to step forward and lead in their major area of knowledge and contribution. Only those who feel insecure and dare not let go for a minute will feel uncomfortable – the 'I decide what we're going to do and then I do it' type of manager, often the unfortunate result of too much emphasis on leadership.

We've all met the glory hound type of manager, always there when the applause is handed out, the first to blame the team when the brickbats are flying. Develop a team of equals and you will shine brighter in the reflected glory of a successful team than from any attempt to hog the limelight of titular leadership. The secure foundation of a performing team reduces stress, increases satisfaction and delivers. Leading such a team is a privilege. But how is this ideal team to be achieved?

The first thing we have to do is put together a complete team. Sounds simple doesn't it? But we may have to start by abandoning a few preconceptions.

HOW NOT TO PUT A TEAM TOGETHER

Everybody believes they know how to put a team together – you just need to make sure you have a player for every position you think you need. Then, of course, you have to be practical and allow for availability of the people you would like, bow to the political realities and, really, you couldn't think of putting a team together for this project without including Henry...

What most people know is how to design a committee, a body that exists to carry out tasks and hold meetings. If it turns out that this develops into a team, that is largely a happy accident. Take a look at the common team assembly approaches:

By *function*

This is how project teams are usually assembled. It's almost as if the people are considered as interchangeable as Lego bricks. Somebody decides that the team will need a designer, somebody from production, somebody to liaise with marketing and somebody from finance to handle the budget and keep things on track. Take them out of the box, click them all together, give them a target, let them set their own agenda, and the job will get done.

One of the pieces is usually leader-shaped and tries to get the rest of the team to fit in with his or her way of working. This is the first reason why two apparently identical teams can be so different in performance: a team lead by a financially biased manager may concentrate on paperwork and reporting; another led by a salesman may break all the rules as long as the end results look OK. This is fine, as long as the followers are prepared to conform to the leader's style and direction. Sometimes it works out well, particularly if things run smoothly. It's when the pressure is on and the stress creeps in, when the deadline is going to be missed or the budget is running out, and in particular when it looks as though someone is going to have to take the blame, that this team begins to fall apart.

Now look at a management team assembled the same way. Often under pressure, with potential conflicts of interest, each member committed to their function: the sales director thinks the finance director too cautious; the development director thinks the managing director is pushing too hard; the production director wishes that the sales director would stop changing priorities; the marketing director wants everyone to keep to the plan.

If things are going badly, this team can degenerate into a finger-pointing, points-scoring, fault-finding mess. Stressful for the team and for those who work for them as they try to cope with a power group who pull in several directions at once. Even when they are going well, problems with behaviour and communication style can result in contributions being undervalued or discounted.

Function is merely a crude net with which to trawl for team members.

By *workload*

Most single function teams – sales teams, work study teams, development teams, are assembled on this basis. They grow in size according to the ambition and political skill of the appointed leader, who gets others to agree that his team needs more resources to cope with the real or imagined workload. All too often this is simply an empire builder's charter.

The team working factors which make the team a success are ignored. New appointments and new teams are created by looking for people who most closely match the team manager's definition of a successful member. This is often on the basis of, 'Are there any more at home like you (or even like me!)' This is not always detrimental to performing the single function of the team. However, teams formed on this basis tend to isolationism and to 'them and us' thinking in the wider team context of their support services and the needs of the rest of the organisation.

The leader of this single function unit, and his deputy (if he or she has one) need to be well integrated into the surrounding parent organisation, or what usually happens is that one of the subordinates sets out to beat the system and takes over their role in the wider company team (eg the salesman based near head office, who can always get a special delivery and whose orders are jumped to the front of the queue).

For *harmony*

This happens more often than you'd think, when people decide that all interests must be represented. It usually works on the basis of 'We mustn't leave Henry out if we are going to ...'. This implies that, whatever you wish to do, if Henry is not included he will sit around firing torpedoes.

But Henry often has his own agenda which has nothing to do with the team's stated goals. So Henry may treat the team as just one more pawn in his power struggle with the management, or just play dog in the manger. Either way, it's instantly fatal, mainly because the rest of the team know exactly why Henry's there, so they all pay lip service to his ideas and then work round him. Henry gets miffed and fires the torpedoes anyway. (With apologies to all those called Henry, but we have found that almost every organisation has their Henry.)

Pick a leader

Very British, upper lips stiffen automatically: 'All the chaps need is leadership and they'll be fine.' No they won't, not if they're any good! Individuals will still want to do things their way, often in conflict with the leader or each other. The leader then either does it his way, ends up as a referee, or is simply isolated. Some team members just opt out. For one thing, if this team succeeds the leader gets the credit. If it fails, the team (or somebody in it) will be the scapegoat. Everybody knows this, so it's Him and Us right from the starting gun.

The leader can become isolated or isolate himself. You hear phrases such as 'You can't manage if you're too close', 'It's the loneliness of command', as if the leader was alone on the bridge of a destroyer, gazing steely eyed into the teeth of an Atlantic gale. As a National Coal Board Mine Manager, who had been battling with Arthur Scargill and the National Union of Mineworkers during the seventies and early eighties, said to us on one occasion: 'I feel that I should point out that I was not a part of this team. I managed it.'

Frankly, this remote command and control approach goes down like the proverbial lead balloon in the questioning nineties. In the new compressed organisational structures, people expect to be consulted, to participate in decisions and work with more readily than for their boss.

At *random*

It may sound unbelievable, but one fashionable consultancy approach to improving productivity actually creates teams from random groupings. The result is that eight to ten people, made up from a disparate group such as a typist, a storeman, a production line worker, a salesman and some luckless middle manager (who will have to write up their ideas), end up sitting round a table trying to generate some innovative thinking on topics they know nothing about. Similar teams will be doing this all over the company – except for the judges of the output, usually the senior managers, who don't want to impose their ideas.

That this approach occasionally does come up with workable ideas is undeniable. Provided that it stops at this point no harm will be done. It is only when this team is asked to move on from brainstorming to develop their ideas, that one or two people usually end up carrying the rest. They don't really need the rest of this team to do it, although the active core could possibly grow into a real team, if it was given the brief and the necessary time to develop. So the whole exercise just turns one or two more people off what they think is team working.

Charity project teams are also often effectively assembled at random and may well suffer from this approach. The result is usually a BigTeam well into double figures, with a self appointed leader. Responses may vary from 'Good old Joan, she always gets things moving' to 'That Mrs Jones, who does she think she is!' There may well be attempts to form real teams by creating sub-committees. The approach is further hampered by low expectations in terms of contribution: this is voluntary after all, you cannot ask too much of people. Yet, even in the business world, people still go ahead and:

Call for volunteers

Volunteers must be a good thing. They are bound to contribute aren't they? After all they *must* want to do it.

All real teams require a sustained, structured effort to be successful. What happens when the first flush of enthusiasm is over and the time comes round to the long haul of a major commitment?

If the interest was sincere and they can see a fulfilling contributory role for themselves they will continue. If their interest was political it may cease when their personal objectives have been achieved. If they just enjoy volunteering, they will soon volunteer for something else and their effort will be diluted.

By the *rulebook*

Simply following the rule book to create a team accounts for the disparity often seen in two apparently identical management teams or project teams.

There is no reason why a board level team, for example, has to represent all the specialist functions of its business, provided that it can encompass all the tasks required of such a team. The trouble is the unwritten rule book – often applied remotely by financially oriented controlling bodies who want to see a structure they understand – says you have to conform. This is like treating a management team as a football team. It implies that the right number of players will ensure there is a team and ignores the stresses and tensions that may be introduced, particularly if the team becomes unevenly balanced as a result.

After all, sports teams look simple. A football team is a team with the objective of scoring more goals than its opponents. The rule book says it has to field up to eleven members. We all know it has to have strikers, defenders and goalkeepers – you wouldn't dream of putting together a team of eleven strikers!

But it is not that simple in reality. Applying only financial measures to a business, treating the creation of profits on the same basis as creation of goals in a football team, ignores many other factors critical for success. After all, even a successful football team needs a manager to set strategies and tactics, a trainer to keep them up to the mark, a scout to find new players, a physiotherapist to help them recover from injury.

The team of eleven players carries out the executive function for the real team, they produce the team's output, goals! The others complete the team: they plan and direct, obtain resources of players and facilities, maintain and support, monitor and control, motivate and promote. There are additional and necessary tasks that must be replicated in any management team, or it may have the same relevance to its business as a star football team that can't win a match. (That's when they fire the manager, isn't it?)

All these approaches lack one essential element: an approach to team working which starts from what a successful team actually has to *do* to be successful. Any team, at any time, brought together to achieve any desired goal. So it does not matter how good the team looks on paper, you have no way of predicting if it will work as an effective team in practice. We have tried to show you why, whichever approach you take, you cannot just put together those you consider to be the best individuals under your criteria to get a real team. Even if you use methods of analysing and assessing individuals, such as psychological profiling or even graphology, you will not learn how they will actually work in a team environment.

However, when we do decide who will be in our team, we still have to assign the tasks they will carry out. It's time to abandon a few more preconceptions.

HOW NOT TO ASSIGN THE TASKS

Everyone knows how to pass out the tasks – engineers do engineering; accountants work out costs; salesmen sell; buyers buy. Of course, you have to make allowances for the fact that some of the team aren't really up to it, or that 'because of my workload I won't be able contribute as much as I'd like', and then not everyone seems to have the right idea about what needs to be done.

We have all heard the results:

- 'I did it my way.' The team leader took on all the tasks and threw a few crumbs to the team.
- 'Delegation is the key. I delegated, so it's *your* fault.'
- 'Let's split the work by function and report back regularly.' The team meeting ends up as a discussion of what did not get done. People start to miss meetings, other priorities intervene.
- 'Of course, putting Gill and Charlie in the team doomed it from the start.' Individuals will want to do things their way, often in conflict with the leader or each other.

So what is the leader to do? Simply issuing orders kills initiative and reflects an unacceptably authoritarian approach. Yet assigning the tasks is seen as the leader's job. Usually, they are assigned by function in line with what the team member's job title says they are supposed to be. Ability and desire to work in a team is assumed!

This is often a prime cause of low team performance, since the job title defines a cog in a machine, not a person. Besides, if you were trained as a marketeer, are you certain you can tell the difference between an electrical and an electronics engineer in this day and age? You will make assumptions, allow personalities to influence your decisions and be disappointed when things don't happen in line with your expectations. It's also a narrow view, and self-perpetuating. People fight their own functional corner, 'Not me. I'm an engineer, not an accountant.'

Besides, if everybody's just going to contribute to their own task, what's the team there for? To hold meetings? It may look as though everybody's doing what they're best at, but in teams we have helped with our TEAMBuilder programme. The phrase most commonly used to describe a failing team has been: 'There's something missing... We can't quite put a finger on it, but ...' What we often found was not a team but (not again!) a committee.

Leadership courses stress that the leader must make the most of the variety of talents assembled in the team. Fine so far, yet to motivate their best efforts, each team member must feel that their contribution is valued. Praise from the leader (whether due or not) is not enough. Team members must feel within themselves that they have done well and given of their best. All top performing teams achieve this ideal. Yet if contribution by function or job title is not enough what should you do?

As a matter of fact, the engineer might turn out to be quite good at cost accounting, if given the chance. Except that if he is given the chance, the accountant feels threatened – his functional territory is being invaded. He's not telling the engineer about the properties of high tensile steel, is he? So he doesn't want the engineer getting into a detailed cost estimate analysis.

Simply encouraging functional cross over is not enough, unless those concerned recognise the need and can see the benefits to the team. Then the accountant may see another area where his analytical skills can provide an equally valid contribution, or he displays a preference for forward planning, or perhaps he can share in the development of the team's strategy. But how are you to find this out if all you have to look at are the job titles?

It's not even something you are likely to find out at interview and discovering someone has a low 'S' and a high 'I' from psychometric testing rarely takes you any further forward either. Even team oriented tests which measure co-operation v confrontation don't help much. It usually means that the co-operative types end up being loaded down with tasks which they don't like, but feel they can't refuse.

What is needed is an approach based solely on the needs of team working. One that will indicate the real preferences which are being masked by the job titles. The common reaction we get in some quarters on making this statement goes something like this: 'Preferences? You surely don't mean that you can only give people the tasks they prefer? Do you mean to suggest that we can really afford to pander to the personal whims of people when the job *has* to be done by somebody, whether they like it or not!' (Not surprisingly, this statement is usually made by someone who is planning how to pass out the work for others to do.)

Before we go any further, let us ask you two questions:

1. Have you ever tried to assign a task to someone who expressed a preference? (be honest – really tried!)

2. If you have, did you still have some tasks people accepted just for the good of the team?

In these days of workplace matrices, when people may be asked to work in two or more teams, the successful team will be the one whose members, of their own volition, want to do the tasks assigned to them.

Excessive management pressure, coercion, threats, final deadlines, the 'do it or you'll be fired' approach, merely waste people. Stress symptoms appear – lateness, absenteeism, displacement activity and so on. The tougher types just pay lip service and get on with what interests them, or vote with their feet and leave.

In developing the programme outlined in this book over the last ten years we have proved conclusively that, if you assemble a complete team, all the tasks to be undertaken by the team can be assigned to someone who will actually express a preference for the task, including all those tasks you yourself wish to avoid at all costs.

The tasks we all put off are the most basic cause of team failure.

Think about it: teams fail because of the tasks which don't get finished in time. Not because of the tasks that get completed successfully. Why don't we do them? Intellectually we can grasp and agree to the need to do them. Often we volunteer to take them on when we see the effects of not planning or failing to gain the required resources. But they still don't get done consistently as a result of pressure of other work, changed priorities, ran out of time etc, we have all heard the excuses.

Most people will undertake tasks for the team in the short term because they see the need. The difficulty lies in sustaining the level of interest and activity. Thus these excuses can be shown to be of real significance: they are symptoms of the real underlying causes of low performance

What inevitably happens is that it is always easier to find reasons to do those tasks with which we feel comfortable first. We actually prefer to do them. It's not that a team member isn't working, just that they ended up doing different work in the time available, often work for another team whose task assignments were more in tune with the individual. They were still going to do it, when they had the time, it had just had to be put off temporarily.

The concept of a team of equals relies on the premise that if you give a team member a task they prefer to do, they are more likely to do it. Not just well, but also first. Preference is the key that will unlock the power of the team. So the next step is to discover how to assemble a complete team.

HOW TO DO IT: LOOKING AT PEOPLE

A complete team is one that can and does take on and carry out to time all the tasks which a team has to do to be successful. It is not enough for a team to understand that all these tasks need to be done and to agree to do them. Something always seems to get in the way and, for what seems to us perfectly valid reasons, certain key tasks get put off. We're still going to do them, of course... it's quite obvious to everyone that they need to be done... The key words are *a complete team*.

Let's start again. What determines how people work well within a team is not *what* they do, but the *way* they do it; the way they approach everything they do, inside a team or outside it. It's not something they learned at school, at college or during any training they may have had. It's not even something which their past experience has taught them. It's become built into them over time. Most importantly of all, it's something which they are unlikely to be able to change quickly:

We call it their role

Some people are logical thinkers, some are analytical thinkers. Some always look to the future, some seem buried in the old ways and the past. Good salesmen, good negotiators, creative problem solvers, all are recognisable types of person. They all have a unique character.

The key to team development is to study character and then to work at personal relations: Forget about *function* – what people do – and instead concentrate on their *characteristics* – the way they do things. If we're examining a team, it doesn't matter what the team's goal is; in what follows, you can think of organising the production and marketing of a new range of engine oils, doing something about the untidy area on the far side of the car park, or of a family which is fitting out a new kitchen.

In each case it's the characteristics of the people involved which count; or, more accurately, the relative balance of these characteristics in a person. We have given these characteristics names, for clarity. An Innovator, for example, who is a fountain of ideas on the design of containers for engine oil, is very unlikely to have no ideas whatever when it comes to the design of a kitchen. Innovators innovate, no matter what task they're engaged on. Innovation is a characteristic, it's built into them.

It's part of their role

These characteristics transcend job function. They are part of the behavioural make-up of every one of us. Parents, schools, friends, role models, all have had an influence on the way we respond and behave over a long period of time. While certain characteristics are reinforced by job and career choices, (it is unlikely that anyone would succeed in sales without displaying the characteristic we have called Promoter) an ability to innovate, evaluate or plan strategically can be applied to any task, particularly when *assisted* by specialist knowledge or functional skills.

A production manager may well be capable of specifying the requirements of a new line to meet forecast demands for three to five years ahead. Do we automatically assume that the same person is the best person to carry out capital sourcing, negotiating, project co-ordination, engineering evaluation and installation tasks? Sometimes we do and live to regret it, or else we draft in others to help to make up for a perceived shortfall in skill and knowledge on a functional basis. All too often throwing bodies at the problem does not result in any significant improvement. There is a team of sorts to lead, but only one put together as if we were assembling a machine from a collection of available components. The leader is supposed to get them to wear in and fit together.

In developing TEAMBuilder and the team of equals approach, over the past ten years, we have examined many teams. Each was a real team, small enough to need to work at personal relationships (always less than ten people) and dependent on whole team effort for success. Without exception, all the teams in trouble we have worked with were missing out vital team tasks. The team could often see where they were failing – they had checklists, review meetings and even project planning computers – yet still things kept slipping. Leadership alone could not fill this task gap.

To get the team to be successful by getting all the necessary tasks done to time proved to be simple in concept: put together a complete team and then get everyone in the team to contribute to those tasks that match the characteristics which make up their own preferred role.

Most people show combinations of characteristics which give them a primary role and a secondary role and it is quite natural for them to switch between them as circumstances demand. This means that a team of two or three can still function very successfully. However, a few people are polarised in one role – we tend to find them rigid and inflexible.

So what roles do you prefer in a teamworking environment? The next chapter contains a short questionnaire designed to identify your teamworking preferences, together with a score sheet. We suggest that you try the questionnaire before reading further, then once you have identified your primary and secondary team roles, read through the role and characteristic descriptions and advice. **Remember:** There are no right or wrong answers – if you try and fake it you are only asking for the tasks you will dislike!

The teamwork questionnaire is only interested in where you can make your best contribution to a team. There is no team role of leader, boss, manager or supervisor. Being of one role type will not make you more promotable, respected or powerful, but if you are honest with yourself you may end up a lot more productive and happier!

2

Take a Look at Yourself

The first step in moving towards a successful team is to discover the roles you and the rest of the team prefer to play. This is the key to increasing your team working satisfaction and identifying a team identity which will be a secure support at times when the pressure is on.

On the following pages you will see the first few words of a statement about team working, followed by five alternative phrases which might complete it. Please read all the phrases, then rank them in the order in which you believe they reflect the way you would feel or act.

Give 5 points to the phrase which most closely matches, 4 to the next best match, and so on – until you have given a score of 1 to the least appropriate phrase.

There are only two rules:

1. You must not assign the same score to two phrases.
2. You must put a value from 5 down to 1 against ALL five phrases in the group.

We suggest that you use a pencil to mark in your scores in the book. Feel free to photocopy Chapter 2 of this book so that the rest of the team can have a go. After all, you could be very lonely as a team of one!

QUESTIONNAIRE

Remember: Assign 5 points to the phrase which most strongly reflects your preference, 4 to the next strongest, and so forth.

Still can't decide? Why not assign 1 point to the phrase you prefer least and work upwards? The results will still be valid. Do not assign the same score to two phrases in the same group. You must put a value against *all* the phrases – we need to know what you don't like as well as what you prefer!

I make a valuable member of any group because ...

1. I am able to see opportunities for group development, and assign responsibilities to group members – without being too domineering ☐

2. I am systematic in my analysis of the group's goals, and can devise plans to help the group achieve them ☐

3. I can usually lay my hands on the resources the group needs to do its job ☐

4. If I'm given a clear objective, I can be relied on to get on with the job ☐

5. I can spot problems as they arise and show the group how to get back on track ☐

I would usually be invited to join a group because ...

6. I'm good at checking the methods the group uses and make sure that there are procedures covering all major activities ☐

7. I can be relied on to be strong and give direction to other team members ☐

8. I can rapidly estimate what resources the team needs – and what they will cost ☐

9. I can spot good ideas easily and quickly – and get the rest of the group enthused about them ☐

10. I'm good at giving the day-to-day guidance that results in smooth workflow and good working practices ☐

I feel most satisfied when ...

11. Promoting good teamwork and helping the team to work better together

12. Carefully analysing situations, weighing the evidence and drawing conclusions

13. Engaged in work that stretches my creativity and allows full flight to my imagination

14. Using tried and tested methods to produce new output

15. Working out a deal face to face with people who may have something new to offer

When the team is to work on a specific project ...

16. My ability to get the right resources to the right place at the right time eliminates delays

17. My ability to follow instructions and get through the work assigned to me gives the group a fair chance of producing what is needed

18. My vigilance helps the team to identify and hopefully overcome barriers to high achievement

19. My ability to keep the team focused on its goals makes sure it delivers what is expected

20. My care in analysing the goals prevents us missing out activities and procedures

If I were to congratulate myself at the end of a project it would most likely be because ...

21. My ability to budget for the project had ensured efficient use of resources ☐

22. My ability to whip up enthusiasm for the project meant that the team 'cared' about the result ☐

23. My ability to design jobs and organise the work flow kept the group highly productive ☐

24. My ability to identify areas of greatest risk showed the team the best opportunities for improvements ☐

25. My capacity for valid judgment gave the team someone to rely on to make major decisions and give clear direction ☐

My major contribution to teamwork is ...

26. Having good ideas and coming up with novel ways of solving the group's problems ☐

27. Working out the best way of organising the work to minimise wasted effort ☐

28. Getting people to agree on actions that leave everyone satisfied ☐

29. Quickly sensing when people are tense or stressed, and helping them talk through their problem ☐

30. Feeding back to the group information about the extent to which it is achieving, or has achieved, its goals ☐

If asked which part of the work gives me most satisfaction, I would say that I most enjoy ...

31. Observing the group, keeping them on course and performing well

32. Deciding how the group should develop and making sure that it does

33. Analysing goals, assessing risks and choosing the best course of action

34. Making sure that the group has the best materials and equipment with which to produce its output

35. Doing something that is neither too difficult, nor too easy, but which gives me a sense of achievement

I would describe myself as someone who most of the time....

36. Enjoys working with the group to find practical solutions to operational problems

37. Enjoys work that enables me to satisfy my inquiring, investigative nature

38. Likes to exert strong influence on the group's decisions

39. Enjoys work that demands a systematic and thorough approach

40. Enjoys 'selling' ideas, services or products

I'm welcome in group problem solving sessions because of my ability to ...

41. Give and take in my dealings with other team members, though I will try to persuade them to my point of view ☐

42. Maintain a working environment in which the group can freely and openly discuss their views ☐

43. Question the effectiveness and efficiency of each element of the team's activity to identify the real problems and their causes ☐

44. Bring a degree of ingenuity and creativity to group problem solving ☐

45. Fix the agenda and timetable for the activity ☐

Scoring

Enter the score you gave for each phrase into the box of the question number below. We did swap the order of questions around for those people who like to try and beat the analysis!

1	3	7	4	13	1
19	4	25	5	26	4
32	3	38	2	44	1
A	10	B	11	C	8

2	4	8	2	14	3
20	2	21	4	27	5
33	4	39	4	45	2
D	10	E	10	F	10

3	1	9	1	15	2
16	1	22	1	28	3
34	1	40	1	41	4
G	3	H	3	I	9

4	2	10	5	11	4
17	3	23	2	29	1
35	5	36	3	42	3
J	10	K	10	L	8

5	S	6	3	12	S
18	S	24	3	30	2
31	2	37	S	43	S
M	12	N	11	O	12

Your scores should now show as three entries in each block column. Add the totals of each column. This gives you your preference score for each of the characteristics which go together to make up one role.

Now transfer each characteristic total to the role boxes (overleaf): totals A, B and C under Driver. D, E and F under Planner and so on. The scores for your preferences now link to the characteristics' names, which combine together to form the role. Add the totals for the characteristics together to get your role scores. You may find it helpful to fill in the little boxes with a cross so that you can see a bar chart of your preference profile. One point equates to one section – the maximum possible characteristic score is fifteen.

When you have worked out all the role totals, check that they add up to 135 – if they don't you have lost or gained a few points somewhere. Have you assigned the same score to two phrases in the same question group of five?

You may find it helpful to highlight the two roles (e.g Planner and Enabler) which show the your highest scores. The highest score is your **primary** preferred role, the second highest score your **secondary** role (eg you may come out as a Driver/ Enabler or a Planner/Exec – any combination is possible.)

Do you have a third role which scores more than 30? Highlight that one also. It is more likely that you only show the occasional high characteristic score (eg Auditor or Monitor) in other roles. Highlight any characteristic score outside the primary and secondary roles which scores greater than 10 (ie 11–15).

Take a copy of your score sheet and keep it with you as you go through the book, it will save you flipping pages later when you forget whether the Monitor is a Controller characteristic or belongs to the Exec. It also makes a handy bookmark!

ROLE SCORE SHEET

		1 2 3 4 5 6 7 8 9 10 11 12 13 14 15
A:	DEVELOPER	
B:	DIRECTOR	
C:	INNOVATOR	
	DRIVER	

		1 2 3 4 5 6 7 8 9 10 11 12 13 14 15
D:	STRATEGIST	
E:	ESTIMATOR	
F:	SCHEDULER	
	PLANNER	

		1 2 3 4 5 6 7 8 9 10 11 12 13 14 15
G:	RESOURCE MANAGER	
H:	PROMOTER	
I:	NEGOTIATOR	
	ENABLER	

		1 2 3 4 5 6 7 8 9 10 11 12 13 14 15
J:	PRODUCER	
K:	COORDINATOR	
L:	MAINTAINER	
	EXEC	

		1 2 3 4 5 6 7 8 9 10 11 12 13 14 15
M:	MONITOR	
N:	AUDITOR	
O:	EVALUATOR	
	CONTROLLER	

To find out what all this means, turn to Chapter 3. We suggest that you take a good look at your own roles and their characteristics first, then read through the other roles – who would fill them on your team?

3

The Five Team Roles

You should now know your preferred and your secondary team roles, and have seen the task based characteristics scores which combine to form the roles. Before you look in detail at the role information which follows, we thought we should let you see the thinking behind them which went into their development.

In simple terms the roles which will create a successful team have been engineered. Much of the work was based on earlier theoretical studies, which led us to look behind the job titles and concentrate on how people worked in the team. To us the academic approach had only one weakness – it appeared in many cases to concentrate too heavily on why teams fail. So we took the pragmatic engineer's approach: find out what works then duplicate it and, if possible, refine it. The first step was to analyse successful teams and to find out what they were doing to be successful. This work resulted in identifying 15 task categories, which every team had to work at to be successful.

Once everyone knows what they have to do, we all thought, they can all get on with it and succeed. But of course they didn't. There were tasks which, while everyone accepted they should be done, were still somehow not getting done. The reasons seemed perfectly valid: time pressure, other priorities, lack of this or that resource. You could take two seemingly identical teams in terms of specialisation and see a different pattern of tasks which were being done successfully. We needed an additional tool to identify why those differences occurred. The cogs were all being put in the same place but the gears weren't meshing in the same way.

A formal psychological approach provided the key. We discovered that those people who did the tasks well and on time for the team had one factor in common – they preferred doing those tasks! We then checked from the other direction: what were the tasks they didn't get finished on time, even though in many cases they had volunteered to do them? They were the tasks they could do if pressed, but had little desire to do in practice. They were a chore rather than a pleasure to the person concerned. So something else always came up – they were still going to do it, but the doing was usually put off until the pressure to produce something (anything!) was unbearable.

From this apparently simple basis, the 15 behavioural characteristics used were identified and developed. If some of the tasks related to these characteristics are left undone, the team will be low in performance. As our experience grew and we refined the process, these 15 characteristics were found to form natural groups. We call these groups of characteristics, **roles**.

There are only five roles to understand. This is based on the practical premise that a role is useless if you can't remember what it means! We found, as the Romans did with the maniple (five fingers/five people – the basis of the Roman legion), that five is a very effective communication group. Particularly when you consider that people aren't that predictable – nearly everyone has a secondary role preference which comes to the fore at times.

All this, remember, is in a team of less than ten people. Everyone must have a role to play. In a real team, you can't afford to leave anyone out! This does not mean that you will automatically have a full set of roles in your team – we will cover what to do about that in Chapter 7.

But why have roles at all? Surely they are just labels? All language is based on naming things – that is how we communicate with one another. When we go to a team meeting we are already wearing a label: one that says Engineer or Accountant. Unfortunately these function names separate people into limited positions which ignore the needs of team working. We found that we needed to remove the function labels so that people can work together as a team.

The teamwork questionnaire is only about teamwork preferences, not about personality, ability or skill. It is only about showing those you work with those tasks you would prefer to do for the team. When everyone on the team is aware of each other's preferences they will have a new and more reliable way of assigning and accepting tasks for the team.

So role preference is not related to function, job title or performance. This is not an assessment of capability, only of preference – working on the premise that if a role is preferred you will probably be more effective in tasks which fit the role (and can also avoid the ones you dislike!).

Role preference lets the others in the team know how you see yourself. It has nothing to do with the external labels we all carry or one's position in the hierarchy. You will see that there is no team role of leader. We look on *leadership* as a functional task, as is *management*. It is perfectly possible to lead from any role.

Of course, this will give a leader a fresh insight into how the team works. Matching each task to the person who is most suited to it by role preference will make it more likely to be done well. In addition, each team member should find their tasks more fulfilling. Assigning tasks out of role context is a major cause of poor team performance and *stress*.

Each of the five roles must be taken on by someone in the team. This can mean having two roles, or role sharing.

- **Driver** – develops ideas, directs and innovates.
- **Planner** – estimates needs, plans strategies and schedules.
- **Enabler** – the fixer – manages resources, promotes ideas and negotiates.
- **Exec** – the producer, co-ordinates and maintains the team.
- **Controller** – records, audits and evaluates progress.

All successful teams contain members who fulfil these roles – even a team of two!

The scoring boxes build up to show you your preferences for each role by its behavioural characteristics. For example, the Planner role combines the Strategist, the Estimator and the Scheduler. The scores are combined for the three characteristics which make up each role and the highest combined score identifies the preferred role under favourable conditions.

This is your primary preferred role. The next highest score is your secondary preferred role. (You may already be picking up this role for your team, as and when the need arises.)

If you end up with two roles with the same score, don't worry. This simply means that you will switch seamlessly between one or the other as the situation demands. From our research into role comfort, the role displayed first in the listing tends to hold a slight margin of dominance over those further down, so if you are evenly balanced as a Driver/Enabler, the Driver will probably come marginally to the fore.

The next sections will tell you about the roles, give you broad *action* and *guard* points for the role, then look in more depth at the characteristics, giving you task based suggestions for you to develop in your role for the team.

In addition you will see a section on Out of Role Performance. This will show you how you are likely to approach role and/or task areas outside your primary or secondary roles. This may happen if you act in leadership mode and *unconsciously* try to plug the gaps you see in your team. Or you may simply be asked to take over a single function team and try to relate to the required role: eg act like an Enabler when taking over a buying team, when you are really a Controller. Far better to look around and assign the tasks within a role, even if it means someone stepping forward in their secondary role.

We suggest that you read your own primary and secondary role descriptions first, then look at the other roles which make up a successful team.

DRIVER

Drivers are intuitive decision makers. They use their instinct to reach conclusions rather than make a detailed analysis of a situation. Detail is the last thing they are interested in.

Drivers love change. If there isn't enough exciting change going on they will try to instigate some of their own. They like life in the fast lane and will rush to overtake those they consider slower movers, occasionally trampling them in the process without noticing.

Their's is a forward looking role. They create a vision of a required future and insist that everyone works towards it. As they prefer to 'tell' rather than 'sell' their vision of the future, they often have problems getting everyone else to run at what they consider to be the right speed in the right direction.

The Driver can see 'big picture' opportunities, and assess 'bottom line' benefits. They look at the big numbers and aim for the big objectives. As a result they tend to be risk takers who rely on speed and quick reactions to succeed. If there is a major decision to be made in the team, it is usually the Driver who is first to make it.

Drivers are enthusiastic organisers and team developers and they will insist that the team be prepared to grasp the opportunities presented. Problems which face the team are meat and drink to the Driver, who acts as a problem solver and catalyst for improvement, to make the team a better place to work.

Action and guard points

If you want to 'grow' in the Driver role you must combine the Developer, Director, and Innovator. Try to:

■ make major decisions for the team;

■ set objectives for team tasks and development;

■ establish directions for team development;

■ assign responsibilities to team members;

■ get the team moving;

■ think growth – People – Skills – Influence – Team Maturity.

Drivers have their weaknesses – be on your guard! To counter the common Driver teamworking problems, be sure to:

■ Listen to ideas and criticism from other members.

■ Don't just drive; check progress, resources and skills.

■ Resolve details as well as the big decisions.

■ Think role – not function.

■ Take more time over people.

The Driver role encompasses three forward looking characteristics for the team: the Developer, the Director, and the Innovator.

Developer

The Developer identifies directions for the team. They clarify the opportunities, describe their vision of the future and the strategy for getting there. It is the Developer who ensures that the team grows along lines that best suit the chosen direction. Growth which leads towards a healthy, mature team with sound goals: eg, by encouraging greater openness and less 'finger pointing' when errors occur.

The Developer also tries to build the team's power and influence so that when opportunities do arise, the team gets the chance to go for them – *and* works hard to build their confidence to do so!

To improve as a Developer, you help the team to grow: get to know what makes a strong team; try to predict what the future may hold, and what the team will need in order to succeed.

■ Make a list of all the changes to be tackled by the team over the next three months. Discuss with the Planner and pick one to work on.

- Pick three contacts who could enhance the team's influence and arrange to talk over the team's future with them.

- Take the time to get team members to talk about their team problems.

Director

Directors are usually dissatisfied with the way things are done at the moment. They see improvement as a challenge and change as normal. If there isn't enough of a challenge within the team, they will seek it outside. It is the Director who breaks down the barriers to progress, like: 'We've never done it that way' or 'Very interesting, but it wouldn't work here'. In fact, if there is a new way of doing something the Director usually wants the team to use it.

The Director gets things done – usually by others! They originate action and transform the working of the team. They will demand, instruct, urge, coerce and challenge in order to get what they want done.

To improve as a Director, you help the team to make its major decisions: you recognise when a decision is needed; make the 'best' decision; and get the decision implemented.

- List five problems, present and future, needing a decision. Get the Controller to provide a full analysis of the background factors before making a decision.

- Talk to the Planner about ways to improve the forecasting of decision outcomes.

- Carry out a strategy review and involve the rest of the team.

Innovator

The Innovator is the corner-stone of the team's creative effort. Innovators are imaginative and ingenious, and dedicated to discovering ways of making the team more effective, in all that it does.

The Innovator is a catalyst for the team: sets the team's sights on new opportunities, introduces new methods and provides impetus to get going. They add to the cohesive force that binds the team together, but not by being a person interested in people as people. Improving methods makes the probability of team success greater.

Improving individual and team performance makes teamwork more attractive and membership a privilege.

The Innovator produces the original solutions to the team's problems that make these improvements possible. Innovators speed the process of change. To grow as an Innovator, try to develop your problem solving skills. Concentrate on data to predict possible outcomes and develop solutions.

- Pick one future opportunity and make a list of the improvements, technical and/or personnel, the team needs most to go for on it.

- Define the team's most important current problem with the Controller and get the team to brainstorm its possible solution.

- Identify one new tool or technique that would enhance the team's performance, and work out how best to use it.

Out of role performance

This looks at the distortions which are likely to occur when a Driver attempts to adopt another role to plug a gap they perceive in the team, especially if this role bears no relation to their secondary role preference.

Planner: The signs of a Driver operating as a Planner are easy to see: a Driver's plan will have only one or two target dates on it – usually set far enough away as to make them seem feasible! As for the detailed planning out of the work programme, the Driver has a vision of what everyone is supposed to be doing and expects the rest of the team to get on with it – they can work out the detail as they go.

Interestingly, many successful Drivers also display a strong preference for the Strategist characteristic. They have learned that they have to explain their vision of the future as a strategy the team can understand. They are still not interested in determining if the strategy is feasible or in scheduling the tasks realistically.

Enabler: A common secondary role for the Driver, often moved to from the primary role when under pressure. At this stage the Driver will start to promote his or her ideas after rejection at the first attempt.

A Driver attempting the Enabler role will get into too many head-to-head situations. The Enabler is more flexible and negotiates to achieve a 'mutual win' scenario. The Driver just wants to win. The Driver will use influence to get others to find and obtain needed resources, the Enabler would use their own network and get them faster. The Driver will promote, but use their own intuitive logic rather than make it attractive or exciting in the Enabler way.

Exec: A Driver/Exec can be a loner's role combination. As one young Driver described it: 'First I decide what we're going to do and then I do it.' In the Exec role, which is all about getting things done and keeping the team together, the Driver will tend to operate well in short bursts, but will not sustain the effort. They tend to pick a task from a characteristic to solve a team problem as they see it:

The team is falling apart under pressure and the Driver will go into Maintainer mode to try and make everyone feel better, but this will be only a flash in the pan – people's feelings are not that important to a Driver. Things aren't coming together, so a spot of co-ordination is tried; if it comes to the crunch, they will sit down and work at a task they consider vital. But, until they see the need again, don't expect a repetition of the task.

Controller: A Driver attempting Controller is a horrible sight to see: they either use the role as a whip to beat those they believe aren't performing, or use it as a barrier to making a decision they disagree with. Occasionally, they pick up the Monitor characteristic, as they see it as a reinforcement of their position. For example, they will take action based minutes, but would omit the record of detailed technical discussion. Drivers are interested in *quality*, but only as far as it enhances their required future. To this end they will often support a Controller against other team members.

PLANNER

Planners are logical thinkers. In their approach to problem solving and decision making, they use their clear thinking to analyse in depth, diagnose in detail and judge with confidence. This is the role which takes the Driver's 'required' future and interprets it into terms and actions the team can understand and use.

Planners look organised, act organised and to their credit *are* organised. They are orderly in the sense of 'a place for everything and everything in its place'; in the sense of having a system or method to get things done; in the sense of preferring to establish and adhere to the rules. They are more comfortable with regular procedures and tend to be conservative in their approach to change. They may, in fact strongly resist any attempt to change their way of doing things or the environment in which they do them.

Planners are forward looking. They project from both past performance and present operations, to outline the aims for the future. Planners are analysts: when decisions are needed on what must be done, and how well, the Planner sets the targets. They will do their best to accommodate other people's needs and be open minded to their views – until the plan is accepted. After which they expect it to be followed and defend it strongly.

The Planner always looks for points of potential failure when laying out plans, in order to build in courses of action that will make success more certain.

Planners set very high standards for themselves in each of their activities and they work hard to achieve them. They set equally high standards for others and they are, perhaps, in the best position to know what others should be doing.

Action and guard points

If you want to be good in the Planner role you must combine the Strategist, Estimator and Scheduler. To contribute you should:

- take the team's strategic aims to bits, get to know them thoroughly;

- assess the environment in which these aims must be achieved. Consider:
  – the team that you have now, and
  – the support that you will get;

- set concrete goals and realistic performance targets;

- expect problems, but try to anticipate them. Take steps to prevent them, but also plan how to respond if they occur.

Planners have their weaknesses – be on your guard! To counter the common Planner teamworking problems, be sure to:

- Stay in touch with your plans to their completion. Don't give the impression you've skipped!

- Allow for contingencies, but don't tell outsiders it will take twelve months, and give the team six; be realistic.

- Don't spend so long looking for dangers that you become immobilised. A certain level of risk is essential.

- Accept the information you get as the plan proceeds and use it to improve future planning.

Strategist

Strategists put flesh on the Drivers 'required' future. They take what could be a loosely defined aim and develop it into a detailed strategic statement.

Strategists visualise the organisation needed to achieve the aim, how to build it, and the effect it will have on the people involved. They are able to link what has gone before with what the future may hold, so they are able to see what might go wrong. Seeing the threats that lie in wait, they design the appropriate defences. It is the Strategist who draws up the actions the team must take to achieve its aims.

To grow as a Strategist, try to develop your skills in finding, analysing and presenting the right information to define the routes to the team's goals.

- Describe the team's primary goal, devise a strategy to match it and get the team to accept it.

- Make a short list of people from the areas with which the team interacts, and persuade them to input to the team's planning activity.

- Discuss with the team those parts of the plans they believe can't possibly be changed and get them to explain why.

Estimator

The Estimator examines in detail the way the team currently operates. This could involve research into the different kinds of task done by the team.

In this way, the Estimator assesses how much work the team is capable of doing and, by interpreting the strategy, the capacity likely to be required. It is the Estimator who analyses the strategic goals to determine what resources the team will need, whether they are already available, or whether the team will need to acquire additional resources.

To grow as an Estimator you should try to develop your skills in determining the political, social and technical feasibility of the team's plans.

- Analyse the team's plans and make a list of the resources needed to achieve them. Discuss with the Enabler how best to obtain them.

- Talk with the Exec about the way the team operates. Make a list of the areas likely to need improved procedures, increased skills or more work.

- Pick a recently completed task and work out if the use of additional resources at the right time would have cut costs. Check the information with the Controller.

Scheduler

Schedulers analyse the tasks to be performed by the team to achieve their strategic aim. They will work out which tasks are best suited to each role and which activities must be combined and allocated as a single job function.

The Scheduler will identify which tasks must be performed in sequence and when tasks can be performed in parallel. The Scheduler will tell you when team members should work together, determine what resources are needed and identify when and where they will be required. It is the Scheduler who creates the timetable for tasks to be performed and plans the acquisition and use of resources.

To grow as a Scheduler, try to develop your skill in determining what needs to be done, in what order and for how long – and the effect this will have on team members!

- Break down the key team tasks that must be done over the next month into those jobs which must be done in sequence and those that can be done at the same time.

- Make a list of all the deadlines. Against each item show the effect on the plan if the deadline were missed. Get the Exec to indicate problem timings.

- Produce a timetable for achieving the team's goals. Get the Controller to include it in the progress control diary.

Out of role performance

This looks at the distortions which are likely to occur when a

Planner attempts to adopt another role to plug a gap they perceive in the team, especially if this role bears no relation to their secondary role preference.

Driver: Planners are naturally cautious and reserved in their decision making. Concern over what could go wrong weakens and delays the Planner's decision making, although once they have been convinced by the facts and a decision has been taken, it will require a detailed case to change it. Planners are problem staters rather than problem solvers and their desire to minimise risk will tend to make them lean towards the logically justified solution in place of the more innovative creative leap.

Enabler: While not inarticulate, the Planner seldom generates the fluency of the Enabler. As resource managers, they have information based networks, rather than sources of supply. When negotiating, they tend to get stuck on points of detail.

Exec: A concern over the tasks to be done tomorrow, can get in the way of the tasks that need to be done today. The Planners social needs are weaker, so that the Maintainer characteristic may be ignored. However, the Exec is a common secondary role for the Planner, co-ordination and production being seen as natural extensions of the planning tasks.

Controller: The Planner shares an attention to detail with the Controller. Both roles need to 'dot the i's and cross the t's'. The Planner's analysis is used as a basis for determining future courses of action. The Controller is interested in the past for its own sake. In the Controller role, the Planner will monitor, but the auditing and evaluating areas may tend to be weak, leading to a low emphasis on quality issues.

ENABLER

Enablers rely on their personal values to direct their decisions. Enablers are natural 'sales' people. They will work hard to convert people to accept their point of view. They are outgoing, persuasive and friendly and will use their capabilities to 'sell' the team new ideas and to promote the team to the rest of the organisation.

Enablers are enthusiastic acceptors of anything new. They are fast to take up a new idea, but if a 'better' one comes along, they may drop the first with equal alacrity. The Enabler will take a new plan and make sure that the team gets all the available resources (including people with appropriate skills) to follow it through.

They are comfortable in one-to-one relationships and can meet strangers with assurance and ease. They converse well and take pains to make others feel at ease, while competing in business in a friendly and optimistic manner, though they are not always well organised.

To achieve their aims, they will prepare a strong case, but are not rigid and so will also negotiate well for the team.

Action and guard points

If you want to be good in the Enabler role you must try to combine the Resource Manager, Promoter and Negotiator. Try to:

- acquire the best resources available;

- identify how resources have been used in the past and make sure they are used better in the future;

- develop the knowledge, skills and attitudes of team members;

- use every opportunity to motivate team members and excite the rest of the organisation;

- note what you give to and receive from your network of contacts, you never know when you will need to call in a favour.

If you want to be a successful Enabler you should guard against the common Enabler problems. Be sure to:

- Balance the availability of training with the work demands of team members.

- Stick to one 'future' at a time, don't rush off in all directions.

- Be prepared to give something when bargaining for resources.

- Identify what it is that the other person wants; even successful negotiators sometimes assume that the other party wants the same thing they do.

Resource Manager

Resource Managers understand the nature of the resources needed by the team, how they are used and how they are controlled. They are best at identifying and acquiring those resources (material, equipment, space, sponsorship and so on) the team will need for future activities. They will be the one who notes any problems in getting the resources the team needs and updates the Planner.

Resource Managers recognise the sort of team they are trying to build. They create job specifications from the Planner's output and highlight the personnel needs that result. They consider the personal development of team members required by the team's plans, and identify the appropriate sources of training and skills development.

To grow as a Resource Manager you should try to develop your skills as a 'Mr Fixit'; both to acquire material resources, and to get the right people.

- List the resources (materials, information, equipment, facilities, people) needed for a current task – what can you do to make it easier to get them?

- Get the Exec to list critical shortages. Pick one item and find a way to improve matters.

- List the problems met when recruiting and selecting team members. Pick one problem and find a way round it.

Promoter

Promoters publicise the team's successes both to the team, and to those outside it. They are the team's natural 'sales' people, who 'sell' the team to everyone around it, just as they 'sell' the team's plans and its future to the members.

Promoters highlight the team's goals and strategies and communicate these hopes and directions clearly, so others understand them. They raise the team's enthusiasm and increase their determination to achieve the chosen goals.

Promoters overcome resistance to change by showing other team members that their personal interests will be best served by following the team's plans for the future. To grow as a Promoter you should try to develop your communication and persuasion skills, and recognise the network of key people who you must persuade.

- Go and talk to the people affected by a team decision and try to convince them of its merits. If in doubt as to the most important people to influence, talk to the Driver.

- Write an outline of key points in a current task that will help you persuade everyone of the team's value.

■ Make a list of the arguments in support of the team's planned strategies.

Negotiator

The Negotiator gives the team a realistic view of the outside world. They are best at forming a clear picture of the people with whom the team must negotiate; who may help and who could block the team's progress. The Negotiator identifies what people expect from the team, and how satisfied they are with what they get. It is the Negotiator who makes proposals for improvements to the team's output to satisfy external needs.

The Negotiator bargains for the team's resources. To do this well, they show both sides how they can achieve their aspirations, help to mediate between conflicting views and smooth over ruffled feelings.

To grow as a Negotiator you should try to develop your skills in setting achievable objectives, solving problems, and at building your stamina!

■ Choose a situation where the team's interests differ from a supplier's. List what you must get, should get, and are willing to concede in a negotiation.

■ Get the Controller to describe the most boring part of the team's work. See how long you can go before you finish one of the sentences. This can be the best listening practice you will ever get!

■ Choose an important question and work out what will happen to the team if you say 'yes', or if you say 'no'.

Out of role performance

This looks at the distortions which are likely to occur when an Enabler attempts to adopt another role to plug a gap they perceive in the team, especially if this role bears no relation to their secondary role preference.

Driver: The Enabler in this position is more likely to take the time to generate apparent consensus and may thus appear weaker than a true Driver. They will grab at an exciting new idea, but are less likely to develop original solutions of their own. Only in the Developer's tasks will they feel relatively comfortable, as the resource manager has a similar interest in finding ways for team members to develop.

Planner: Enablers are strongly tactical in their approach and have little interest in strategy which they regard as a theoretical constraint on what they want to do now. If they plan the work, they are unlikely to stick to the plan. A shrug of the shoulders and an admission that 'I got it wrong' will be used as a basis for doing something that appeals more strongly at the time.

Exec: Only in those tasks which relate to areas of communication is the Enabler going to shine. They will put in a lot of hard work preparing to communicate, but don't take this as an indication that they will sustain a more typical Exec task. As a Maintainer they are poor counsellors – they don't spend enough time listening and are far too ready to talk about their own experiences.

Controller: Enablers consider the Controller's role to be a source of bad news. Pushed into it they will look for the good things, but tend to cut out the bad news as irrelevant, unless they are forced to analyse a major disaster which can't be ignored. The most damaging result is that the Controller's early warning systems go missing, as an Enabler will neglect to keep the necessary records. Don't ask an Enabler to take the minutes; they get so involved in the meeting they forget to write anything down for long periods.

EXEC

Execs base their decisions both on observation and on how they feel about what they see. Execs are realists: they are not unduly influenced by the 'Big Picture' or the fine detail. A job needs doing, so they get on and do it. They are capable of turning instruction into action, systematically, patiently and completely, aligning and interlocking individual plans and tasks in pursuit of a shared objective.

Execs live in the present and recognise what needs attention *now*. They are little influenced by what has gone on in the past and don't worry too much about what the future may bring.

It is the Exec who makes the effort to ensure that the team works in harmony to get things done. They help people to recognise the nature of their problems, to gain insight into the way to solve them, to find solutions and to put them into effect.

Action and guard points

If you want to develop in the Exec role you must combine the Producer, Co-ordinator and Maintainer. To contribute you should:

- handle the team's administrative tasks;
- make sure that team members have work to do and systems with which to do it;
- identify the knowledge, skill and attitudes the job demands;
- balance the work to be done and the ability to do it;
- maintain good relations between the individual team members.

Execs have their weaknesses – be on your guard! To counter the common Exec teamworking problems, be sure to:

- Show people the daily achievements, it's all too easy to be seen as a plodder.
- Be open about team problems, and actively help to solve them.
- Check that the team still has a reason to exist before spending too much time keeping it together.
- Make sure that help is needed before you give it.
- Lift your head from the task occasionally to see where the team is going.

Producer

Producers turn plans and instructions into action. It is the Producer who generates the team's output, whether it is a product or service. Given a job to do and the resources with which to do it, the Producer will perform. Producers are goal-setters and goal achievers, but they are realists. They will not try to achieve the impossible.

Producers need a system to operate or a procedure to follow. If there isn't one, the Producer will create it. They participate in job design and organising work flow and develop the technical skills, the flexibility and the resilience to do the jobs the team is given.

To grow as a Producer you should try to improve your skills in job design, goal setting and procedure writing.

- What was your greatest contribution to the team's work over the last six months? What made it a success? How could you do it even better next time?

- Set yourself the personal goal of redesigning those team procedures with which you are unhappy. Make sure you discuss them with the Roles most involved.

- Select the vaguest instruction the team has received recently. Rework it to make it complete and unambiguous. Test it on the team to see if you have succeeded.

Co-ordinator

Co-ordinators are best at balancing the varied and often conflicting demands placed on the team by different parts of the organisation. The Co-ordinator makes sure that each team member has a fair share of the day-to-day work and that individual tasks are aimed at achieving the same team goals.

Co-ordinators develop and regulate the team's standards of behaviour. They are also more likely to criticise non-conforming behaviour. It is the Co-ordinator who organises the individuals and fuses them into a working team.

To grow as a Co-ordinator you should try to develop your skills in maintaining the work flow despite conflicting demands on the team's time.

- Identify a bottleneck in the team's work flow, ask the Controller's help in analysing causes and work out a way to get things moving again.

- Keep the team informed of current achievements and try to build on them to improve performance.

- List events during the past three months that have badly affected the work of the team. Identify those where nothing has been done to prevent it happening again; work with the Planner to build safeguards.

Maintainer

Maintainers hold the team together. They are the natural counsellors of the team. Maintainers spot conflict early in its development and help those involved to clarify and resolve the issues. It is the Maintainer who helps people to recognise the nature of their problems and gives insight into the ways they may solve them.

Through counselling, they help all team members set realistic goals and workable strategies to solve problems of team relationships. They give continual support, as team members attempt to resolve their conflicts, solve their problems and talk over their progress and results.

To grow as a Maintainer you should try to develop your skills in counselling to prevent and manage conflict and ease the team's relationships.

- Pick a recent event when the team failed to agree. Get those involved to talk through possible solutions, first with you and then together.

- What would you like to see from a planned change? Talk to team members about your feelings and try to get them to do the same to identify any source of conflict.

- List the problems that have occurred when introducing a new team member. How would you prevent them happening again?

Out of role performance

This looks at the distortions which are likely to occur when the Exec attempts to adopt another role to plug a gap they perceive in the team, especially if this role bears no relation to their secondary role preference.

Driver: Decision making is a very stressful activity for the Exec. They will seek support to the point of appearing to ask other team members to make the decision, but don't be surprised if they reject both the advice and support and defer the moment. In aspects of problem solving that relate to co-ordination they can perform well, but tend to reject changes in approach as too disruptive and unknown.

Planner: Execs will be strong on producing the plan but weak on the analysis that should proceed it. Strategies which endorse the *status quo* will be preferred. Plan timescales will have a tendency to be extended to make sure that there is plenty of time to get everything done.

Enabler: While they have strong social needs, the Exec is not so comfortable operating outside their circle of acquaintance. Their ability to see another's side to an argument, which makes them invaluable in counselling situations, weakens their resolve in negotiation. The capacity to bear a grudge can mean that, if they believe they have been slighted in some way, communication will break down for a period.

Controller: The obligation to criticise the performance of others makes this role a difficult one for the Exec, although they will happily produce the information required in uncritical abundance. Quality issues that involve tried and tested routines will be handled, but those involving analysis and conclusion will probably be done poorly.

CONTROLLER

Controllers are analytical thinkers. They base their decisions on a careful analysis of what has happened in the past. The Controller is something of a loner at work, but not anti-social. Someone who enjoys developing a detailed understanding of the way the team works, the systems it uses, the real progress it is making and the results it has achieved.

They are able to use their experience and knowledge to give advice and guidance on target setting and on the identification and solution of problems. They will assess in detail the costs incurred by the team's operation and the benefits achieved by it.

The Controllers will spot the team's errors through their careful monitoring of what is going on, and so may well be the main source of information to aid the team's problem solving effort.

Action and guard points

If you want to be good in the Controller role you must combine the Monitor, Auditor and Evaluator. You should:

- decide (with the Planner) how to tell whether the team is making progress towards its goals, and monitor it;

- check that the team is using the best methods to accomplish its goals;

- assess individual performances against objectives and how these contribute to team achievement;

- identify departures from the plan and the accepted level of performance;

- recommend ways to recover from problem situations.

Controllers have their weaknesses – be on your guard! To counter the common Controller teamworking problems be sure to:

- Fit your controls to the person – don't prescribe a way of working without regard to the person (and their role type) who must carry it out.

- Make allowances for those who want to work the 'fast track', they often get the team most of the way. Your controls can then guide the team to a conclusion.

- **Don't** say you can't do it because of the rules, if you make the rules!

- Resist the temptation to let the creation of rules of conduct become your main contribution.

- Don't let your data gathering be used for destructive purposes – you should diagnose symptoms for positive correction, not just furnish ammunition.

Auditor

Auditors analyse the team's activities in considerable detail. It is the Auditor who will check that the resources (material, information, equipment) are of adequate quality to match the activity to be performed. It is the Auditor who will check for errors and, if any are found, will identify cause and responsibility.

This is more likely to be related to systems rather than personnel, unless functional deficiencies show that training is required. Auditors will use their experience to give advice on how the problems might be solved, but are unlikely to take responsibility for solving them.

To grow as an Auditor you should try to develop your skills of observation and quality control.

- Pick a major item supplied to the team with which you are dissatisfied. Was it specified correctly? Was the best supplier used? Did it match the specification? Record your findings and discuss them with the Enabler.

- List sources of training and development. Assess whether they deliver what you want, when you want it, at a price you can afford.

- Assess whether the systems used by the team really work and actively support the team's efforts. If you can, pick one and scrap it without replacement.

Monitor

Monitors produce the team's formal records. They observe the team operation, both in the work it does and as a group of people working together.

Monitors check if the team is following its procedures, and record the results for feedback to the Planner. The Monitor watches over the actions critical to the team's success and records what is effective and what causes problems for feedback to the Developer and the Exec.

Monitors are the team's 'progress chasers'. They know how far the team has got towards its targets, what problems have been met and progress towards their solution.

To grow as a Monitor you should try to develop your skills of observation and recording.

- Discuss with the Planner and Exec the team's plans and deadlines, and the problems of meeting them. Start a team log book to record both failures and achievements.

- Create a progress control diary to record the team's problems, agreed courses of action and the progress towards solution – and use it.

- Identify changes being implemented in the team and record in the team log book how the team reacts to the problems met during the change period. The team log is the key to only making a mistake once!

Evaluator

The Evaluator is the team's judge, at least the internal one. It is the Evaluator who assesses in detail the costs incurred by the team's operation and the benefits achieved by it.

The Evaluator is the team's 'quality manager'. They will report whether the team has provided what was asked for, when it was needed, to the right standard, at a cost within the budget. It is the Evaluator who provides the feedback that will show whether the team's choices were wise, and their efforts truly successful.

To grow as an Evaluator you should try to develop your skills of observation and judgment.

- Pick three end users of the team's output (product or services) and discuss their level of satisfaction.

- Pick a change that was implemented at least two months ago. What has happened? Did it work as intended?

■ List the major activities of the team. Assess whether each still satisfies a need, and does so in a cost-effective manner.

Out of role performance

This looks at the distortions which are likely to occur when a Controller attempts to adopt another role to plug a gap they perceive in the team, especially if this role bears no relation to their secondary role preference.

Driver: The Controller's view of the Driver's decision making tasks can turn him or her into the 'Abominable No-Man'. Being analytical, rather than intuitive, they always require more information before making a decision. Even if all the information available is provided, they may defer on points of presentation of the information. They know what is wrong with the team and will apply the control systems to put it right, often tying the whole team up in red tape.

Planner: The Controller has difficulty leaving the analysis phase of planning, but may produce a workable schedule, based entirely on what length of time things actually took the last time they were done. They will be less effective on exercises which can't look back to a historical base for precedent.

Enabler: A Controller attempting this role will display either extreme discomfort by producing what, to an observer, is a parody of the role, or will stay as Controller and bore you to death. As a negotiator, they will fall foul of points of detail, which may be given a disproportionate emphasis.

Exec: Co-ordination backed by the Monitor attribute will tend to be rigid, but will be done. Work will be meticulous in detail. The social aspect of the role, the counselling and the support which helps hold the team together will, however, be less effective.

4

That's Not Your Role!

At the first team meeting when the group get together after analysing their roles, the first thing everyone says is 'I'm a ..... What role are you?'

The reaction which follows can vary from 'So we're both the same – we'll have to work together more' to 'Never! You a Controller? You always seem more like a Driver to me.'

There are two reasons for this lack of recognition:

- Role Shift under pressure.
- Communication style mismatch.

In a book of this nature, we didn't feel we could subject you to the full panoply of questionnaires which we use in our computer assisted approach. However, there are ways in which, once you know what you are looking for, you can spot those who have either shifted role, or who are masking their real preference – usually in order to conform to the dominant role in a single role team.

HOW PRESSURE AND STRESS CHANGE BEHAVIOUR

Just as you think you have begun to identify and feel comfortable with the various roles in your team, to know that Joe is a Driver/ Enabler and that Mary is a Planner/Exec, there goes Simon, who you all think of as a Driver/Exec, behaving like an Enabler and 'selling' at everyone in sight (and probably doing it badly!).

There will be times in every team's working existence when one or all of the team's members will feel under pressure. The team may respond well – conflict may decrease, decisions get taken faster, changes accepted and the whole apparent running rate increases. Or, just as you feel the need to get going, someone may start to behave untypically, leaving you saying to yourself: 'Why did they do that?'

Pressure is usually the answer. Each of us may reach a point at which we feel the pressure is unacceptable. Pressure is not the same thing as stress. Some of us thrive on pressure and don't really manage – until the deadline is looming – to concentrate the mind.

Under pressure some people keep to their unstressed role. They may appear to be the well balanced core on whom you can rely. But be sure to look at the difference in score between their primary and secondary roles – if the difference is greater than 10 points they may be polarised in that single role. Indeed, there are those who display no clear secondary role at all. As a rule of thumb they will usually have scored over 40 in their primary role and under 30 in other roles. These people may prove somewhat inflexible when it comes to coping with tasks outside the primary role characteristics.

Role shift under pressure

A common response is to shift role type under pressure. A successful team built of equals recognises two types of role shift: one is normally a positive response to pressure, the other is more likely to be a stressful response.

The first, normally positive, response is to move to one's secondary role – we call it a *natural role shift*. Indeed, if the points difference between the roles is 6 points or less this can be as natural as breathing. Although they may appear comfortable with this, you should watch for stress symptoms: increased tension, marked behaviour change (eg withdrawal by a member – unusual silence, lateness, or even absenteeism), sudden antagonism. You can spot the changes at the most basic level once you start to look.

Case 1: Talking to your kids.

Many teenagers fall into the Driver/Exec pattern. 'First I decide what we're going to do and then I do it.' They are not really team players, as they are still developing from the 'Me first, me first!' stage and only co-operate when the task is physically too great to complete without co-operation.

A conversation with one's teenage son might go something like this:

It starts in Driver role – 'Can I go to an all night party?' Blunt and to the point.

'Who are you going with and where is it?'

'In the woods. Everybody's going.' (Still Driver, still the minimum communication.)

Parent raises the pressure: 'I want to know more before I'll agree. I'm not sure I'm too happy about this.'

Unnatural role shift triggered: Enabler comes to the fore and they start to sell you on the idea. Smiling enthusiasm is the order of the day: 'It's well organised. We'll have tents and everything. It's a place where Mark has been with his brothers. Lots of people use it.'

'What happens if your camp fire gets out of control? Who is going to be in charge?'

Pressure is still on. Enabler becomes more subtle. Speech slows to that of a Planner. Body language shows underlying restlessness. 'Stuart could take his Dad's mobile phone... We wouldn't have to have a fire... We'd be careful...'

'OK But mind how you go! When will you be back?'

Pressure is off. Shift back to Driver and give the minimum: 'In the morning. Bye!'

The key points of this example are:

1. Do not be surprised at the rapidity of change – a single sentence can trigger it.

2. Communication style may mask the role shift (see the communication style section in this chapter).

The first role shift may trigger a second spontaneous role shift by another team member at the perceived increase in pressure. This may initiate a domino effect of role shifts as other members move to accommodate the change. The team will feel the stress. Meetings will go round in circles. The same conversations take place again and again.

Case 2: The Role Shift Tango

An initial role shift can trigger a change across the entire team. This is particularly true of incomplete teams, where one or two roles are entirely missing.

In the case of the management team of a design company we studied, the team had recently lost their Enabler, who had gone freelance, and lacked a Controller. The three roles normally present were Driver, Planner and Exec. The team were all designers by training. One of the directors explained:

> Like the majority of medium sized media service companies, we are not run by professional managers. I and my two fellow directors are designers. We knew what we wanted to achieve, but somehow we just weren't achieving it.

The recession in 1990 started to hit design companies hard. The management team held meeting after meeting to try and find a way forward. Overheads had already been cut to the bone.

Role analysis showed that under pressure the Exec shifted role to Driver, this triggered the Planner to move to the vacated Exec slot and the natural Driver to move to Enabler. The shift by the Driver relieved the pressure on the Exec, who switched back, triggering a return by the other two, *but not removing or addressing the underlying causes*.

As they discovered:

> It became clear that we were a team at serious risk from stress and that when we were under pressure we tended to transfer to roles which didn't come naturally to us at all. That meant we were in a vicious circle of piling pressure on pressure – no wonder the team tended to fall apart when we faced a problem.

The solution: Once the problem was recognised the team was halfway there. They gradually learned to stop and review causes, thereby reducing the pressure. In addition, they agreed to share the Enabler and Controller roles, contributing in those characteristics for which they showed a level of preference, to try and create a more rounded team performance.

If you spot a change

You may feel that you should simply ignore it and it will all sort itself out in time. That is what might be termed the polite way. You can hear the thoughts: 'Poor old Jim, off on his hobby horse again,' 'Don't pick up the bricks. Let's change the subject.' and 'This sort of behaviour simply gets us nowhere.'

In a conventionally assembled team you have no real basis for starting the conversation. There would be little point in challenging the change in behaviour, as that would be seen as confrontational and probably be taken as a personal attack by the individual under pressure.

If, however, you all know that these changes can and will occur, surely you can acknowledge that the pressure is rising? The only way to reduce it will be to have the team share some of the load – the essence of teamwork. So don't hesitate; acknowledge their position and try to get them to express their feelings on the matter.

If you see someone go silent and withdraw from the group, it is fair to ask: 'Sally, you're very quiet. What are your feelings at this point?' If you get hit by a barrage of negative criticism from a normally positive character, why not say: 'This certainly throws a new light on things. How do you feel this affects you personally?' If the change is general with no apparent single cause, ask the team: 'Hang on everyone, this is not like us. What has triggered this? Is this a positive change for the team?'

If not – you must intervene and get everyone to step back and review causes. For an individual, it is worth checking on the team member's motives and the effects this change may have on the rest of the team: if the team needs the new role, fine. If the individual needs the new role, because they are overloaded or dissatisfied, check how comfortable they feel in the new role. They may need to sustain it for quite a while – a potential stress point for both them and the team.

Our advice to an individual at this point is always to make it obvious that pressure has triggered the change in their behaviour. Pressure shared can be pressure reduced, particularly if this gets the others to act to reduce the load.

If the whole group has switched, it may suddenly have become a very harmonious place to work. Fred has stopped picking up points of detail, Jenny stopped warning of the consequences, Alec is no longer indecisive, Mary's enthusiasm is curbed and you are all taking decisions at a rate of knots! Leader Brian is over the moon, this is more like it! Before they all congratulate themselves, they should realise that they have fallen into the insidious trap of shifting to a single role team – in this case a team of Drivers. The only thing you can be sure of is that the decisions and agreed actions probably will not stick, but need modification piecemeal later, once everything calms down and the pressure is off. Is this unreal? The stress addict's team below behaved like this all the time!

Try another: Max starts raising points of feasibility, Jane presses everyone to consider the longer term view, Peter stops wanting to do it all by next week, Alan warns of potential points of failure, the pace slows, points are debated in great detail. Leader Jean relaxes, this will get them on the right path. At the end of a long meeting they have identified several promising new areas of research. Which role have they adopted?

Guard against applying too much pressure to achieve consensus, you may only achieve homogeneity of role. The symptoms of this pressure, apart from a move within a meeting towards a common style, is the aftermath: decisions and agreed actions, taken from the viewpoint of a single role, (in the second case above – Planner) are often sent back later for modification or even reversal.

Some people switch to a role which is neither their primary nor their secondary role when unstressed, and this will inevitably lead to the other members of the team misunderstanding them ('She didn't act like this before.'). When team members move to a role other than their secondary role, we call this an *unnatural role shift*.

They may be perfectly capable of taking on the role, but are unlikely to sustain it, as it is not their choice. The role shift may be a correct response to team needs, but can still generate stress. Look at the motives for this role shift:

- If you believe that the team lacks this role, it may be better to discover who shows some interest in it and point out the need to them.

- If it is because the load on *both* the preferred roles is untenable, talk it over with the rest of the team and try to share the load and save everyone some pain.

Since this misunderstanding has arisen precisely at a time when the team may be under stress as well as the individual, it can be extremely dangerous. The individual concerned may not even notice that it has occurred, but if others are taken by surprise, team performance will suffer.

Change within role

There are those whose response under pressure is to change role emphasis: some people accentuate it, others moderate it.

If they moderate their behaviour, it suggests that they believe that, in order to succeed, it is necessary to hold back from behaviour that may be more natural. This holding back is artificial and may cause them some stress, as it could lead to frustration if the pressure is maintained for long enough. The degree of stress will depend on their ability to cope with the pressure. Ask them: Why do they hold back? Watch carefully: Do others respond better when they do?

If they accentuate their behaviour, it suggests that they believe that, for them to succeed, it is necessary to force a level of behaviour greater than their more natural choice. This forcing is again artificial and may cause them some stress, as it will require effort to maintain and may prove wearing if the pressure is sustained for long enough. Ask them why they feel the need to force things. Watch carefully. Can they maintain the pace? Do others respond better when they do?

Case 3: The Stress Addict's Team

There are those among us who only really seem to become human when the adrenalin is flowing. Their affect on a team can be disastrous, especially as the team may feel that they need to respond by role shifting to survive. These people moderate their role polarity under pressure, becoming more role balanced and often bringing forward a secondary role which modifies elements of their behaviour

The team in this case ran a medium sized school in a country district. They represent an archetypical school coping with the changes in education today. They carried into their team situation a history which included a hierarchical background, almost complete independence during the non-team tasks of the day – teaching, preparing and marking lessons etc., and a team leader of high energy who thrived on pressure.

The team was assembled to work on curriculum development and comprised the Head Teacher and three teachers, all of whom had been candidates for the post of Deputy Head.

Our analysis showed that under smooth conditions they had the role potential for a complete team. However, when the team came under pressure, while the Head Teacher moderated his role behaviour and became a more balanced team member, the other team members all made an unnatural (and therefore stressful) role shift to reflect the team leader's role. The effect was that, under pressure, the team all became Drivers.

In this situation, from the leader's point of view, the team may have responded well – conflict decreased, decisions got taken faster, changes were accepted and the whole apparent running rate increased. But *only* during the meetings.

The cost in stress, however, became too high to ignore. In addition, too many decisions failed to get implemented or were brought back to the team in modified form by the Planner, who reverted to role once the meeting was over.

The solution: A slow and careful one for the Leader: to consciously work at his secondary role of Enabler, promoting enthusiasm for tackling the externally imposed problems without imposing Driver decisions *before* a proper examination of alternative courses of action. Not as easy as running a single role team, but far more productive in real terms.

STRESS

Stress is a response to an inappropriate level of pressure. When the pressure gets too great we try to find ways to cope. Coping techniques can include yoga and relaxation, or acquiring skills to overcome a particular source of pressure, such as public speaking.

Moderate or even high stress levels for short periods are not considered harmful and may even be beneficial, enjoyable and necessary. However, even quite moderate stress levels, when continued for long periods are known to be harmful and are thought to be the cause of all sorts of unpleasant and potentially dangerous conditions. Some of these are psychological, ranging from sleep disturbance to full blown neurosis or such conditions as alcoholism. Many are physiological: high blood pressure and duodenal ulcers being the best known, but also include a whole range of effects on the body's immune defence system which are associated with allergies, migraine, asthma and a number of other and more complex diseases which are only just beginning to be understood.

Clearly stress, particularly in the long term, is detrimental. So what can you do about it in a team environment? First you have to recognise the causes: there are two types of stress affecting individuals within the team:

Directed stress comes from outside ourselves – the external pressure and deadlines that every team member faces. It tends to be short-lived and its cause is often obvious. One of the reasons it's thought to be beneficial is that, in fact, we often seek it out and enjoy it – for example indulging in competitive sport, going to noisy pop concerts or riding roller coasters. How often have you heard someone say, quite genuinely, 'I like a bit of pressure, it raises my game', 'I don't really get moving until the deadline's coming up. It concentrates the mind.'

Some people seem to depend on this stimulus of the adrenal hormones to react properly. It may make them feel good, but in a team situation, they can raise the stress of all around them (see Case 3: The Stress Addict's Team).

Non-directed stress occurs when the immediate cause for feeling pressured is not obvious or is unnecessary. Perhaps the most familiar form of non-directed stress is worry.

The phrase 'There's no point in worrying about it,' must be said hundreds of times a day. It is, of course, quite true. If, on your own or part of a team, you are under pressure to meet a deadline, it may make excellent sense to 'over-work' - that is to put in far more hours than you would normally work, even to the point of exhaustion – in order to meet it.

Worrying about it, on the other hand makes no sense at all. You are either going to meet your deadline or you are not. Worrying about whether you will succeed is first of all unproductive (since it directs your energy and attention away from actually getting the work done) but, more importantly, it's a prime cause of long-term stress.

All this can be summed up by saying that there probably isn't any such thing as 'over-work'. What there is always plenty of is 'over-worry'. But there are other, less well recognised sources of non-directed stress in a team situation:

- Role shifts: any of the shifts outlined above may induce non-directed stress in the person who has displayed the shift.

- The actions and behaviour of other people on the team.

Role shifts can be quite dramatic. To help support the team member displaying the shift, and to minimise the knock on stress effects on the rest of the team, try to identify the motivation for the shift:

- *Reversal* is acting the opposite to the way you feel, in the hope that you will start to feel the way you act. For example, putting too much pressure on a supposedly meek and mild person can provoke a startlingly aggressive response, once the adrenaline is triggered.

- *Substitution* is, 'let's do something different and the pain will go away'. This suggests they create their own pressure by simulating a role image under normal conditions, perhaps because they believe it will make them more respected or promotable, but are more comfortable in the substitute role.

Stress is not only bad for the individual but also for the team. In Chapter 6 we will look further at the four causes of team stress and what to do about it.

Communication style

Our communication style determines how we appear to others. Our primary recognition of role comes through speech, rather than behaviour. There are those who go through their business life effectively wearing a communication mask. These are the people whose communication style does not match their role preference. So you should try to look at the behaviour behind the words, in order not to confuse the *appearance* with the *preference!*

Often the internal pressures to conform in a team mean that to be accepted some members feel that they have to communicate in a way which reflects the predominant role type in the group. Drivers and Controllers in management positions are particularly prone to generate this response – although we know of one Driver psychologist who masks his role by communicating as a Planner, so he clearly thinks this is how a psychologist should communicate!

The style descriptions which follow are not just intended to show you how to recognise the roles communicated by other team members. They also show you the way in which others will expect you to communicate to reflect your role preference.

It is time to ask yourself (or the others in the team), do I communicate my role preference? How does everyone else around me really see me? Often the Driver, who has just ridden roughshod over somebody's feelings; has no inkling of how they appear to others. They think they are being entirely reasonable. Similarly, often the Controller who has just shredded the team's confidence and killed its momentum, felt they were applying constructive criticism.

In addition, each role has its opposite with whom they will have the most problems in terms of communicating. Take a fresh look at your role opposite: advice on how best to communicate with them is included in the communication style description for your role. How well do you think you communicate? Do you really get along?

Driver

Drivers use their intuition to make decisions. They are quick to see opportunities, good organisers and full of enthusiasm. They speak quickly, think quickly and move quickly. **But** they often don't give other people enough time to think and reply.

Drivers tend to be blunt and to the point. They don't waste time on detail, though they do demand enough information on which to make their decisions. This may be a lot less than is strictly needed, because they tend to jump to conclusions! They are much happier talking about where the team is going, how well it is doing (they are bottom line people) and actions to improve effectiveness.

It is always the Driver who upsets the sales office or the secretary with what they believe to be a perfectly reasonable request. In reality, the Driver tends to be abrasive and is disinclined to spend time on social niceties. They want to get straight to what is on their mind and will further their required future. They are often impatient and show it and are not afraid of confrontation: as they see it as a way of concentrating the minds of those around them.

Two Drivers in conflict are like two moose in the mating season – they are inclined to head butt each other with what to all around them seems to be a sickening crunch! *But* they will be on to something else tomorrow – they don't take losing to heart and are occasionally ashamed of their actions later. As one famous Driver once put it: 'Ruthless in victory, magnanimous in defeat.' Above all the Driver is a gamesman.

Drivers have most problems communicating with Execs. They find the Exec too laid-back, too difficult to get a genuine, spontaneous response from, hard to get moving and too ready to bear a grudge.

The Execs turn the team's good ideas into practical output – be it a product or service. They are the producers on the team, who need clear instructions and warm words. They want to know what to do, then to be left to get on with it.

Their social needs are much greater than those of the Driver. They need to know they have done well, so make an effort to make Execs feel valued. Any feedback should include due praise. It is important to let them know their effort has benefited other members of the team.

Planner

Planners use logical thinking to evaluate and build on the team's past experience. They assess today's goals, and decide on tomorrow's activities. Their communication reflects this logic and will be clear and precise. But, for some on the team, they talk too deliberately, concentrate too much on detail, are too cautious and too sensitive.

Planners are not naturally aggressive people. They try to avoid conflict if they can, especially on a personal level. They are diplomatic and would rather seek to clarify the situation by asking questions than by making demands. They may, however, end up by walking away from confrontation, leaving each party to go their own separate way.

The Planner thinks carefully before speaking – the pause while you wait for them to respond can be so long you can almost see the wheels going round! This does not mean that they are slow thinkers, they are just trying to be precise. They also expect the same precision of expression from others.

The Planner may appear cautious and find too many reasons not to follow a new direction – all they are doing is checking the feasibility of a course of action. They may need some guidance as to what the team considers an acceptable level of risk. They get very frustrated when, having produced a plan, they feel it is being ignored, but they are also inclined to dismiss the need for change in their last plan as they are already working on the next one!

Planners have most difficulty communicating with Enablers. They tend to find them frivolous, flighty and lacking in perseverance. Planners find the Enabler too optimistic – why can't they see all that could go wrong?' They see them as far too talkative – they don't give people a chance to explain everything!'

When dealing with an Enabler, Planners should remember that they like excitement! Talk about the challenge of the new goal, new strategy, or whatever else is new. They will not stay still long, so prepare in advance and state your requirements in short sharp sentences. But do try not to be dull! Expect to be interrupted – so keep track of where you have got to, and get back on course as soon as you can.

Enabler

Enablers are outgoing, persuasive and friendly. As natural sales people, they work hard to get people to accept their point of view. But they are not always well organised and others may find them frivolous, flighty and lacking in perseverance. Too optimistic and too talkative – they don't always give people time to explain everything!

They converse well and take pains to make others feel at ease. They are comfortable in one to one relationships and meet strangers with assurance, but they do tend to trust and accept others at face value – they must guard against misjudging other people's abilities and intentions.

Enablers wear their hearts on their sleeve. They are not good at hiding their feelings and are often embarrassingly open to relative strangers – in part because they are compulsive communicators. They can always find time to chat and often take a break from what they are doing to go and talk with someone or to make a phone call.

Beware, however the Enabler in Promoter mode. They can be the ultimate method actors, totally believing what they say at the time to achieve their objectives. They will often tell you what they think you want to hear and worry about the consequences later.

Enablers may find it difficult to communicate well with Planners and Controllers. For an Enabler, they talk too deliberately, concentrate too much on detail, are too cautious and too sensitive.

However, this care is their very necessary contribution to the team, so please try to be patient in dealings with them! Both roles need to 'dot the i's and cross the t's' to be effective, so if they seem slow on the uptake, don't let your enthusiasm stop them asking questions. It may take you longer to persuade them than you would like, but they will listen to everything you say and judge it on its merits. Don't waste time telling stories – they don't usually like to be interrupted for a chat. Keep to the point and be prepared for questions.

Exec

Execs live in the present, recognise what needs attention now and apply their experience patiently and persistently. But others may find them too laid back, difficult to get a response from, hard to get moving and too ready to bear a grudge.

Execs speak warmly, they support the team as a whole, and individuals in particular. They form real friendships and will defend their social network. They may sometimes seem slower thinking, because of this strong need to maintain social relationships.

Execs are unlikely to enjoy talking about future changes, which they may find threatening, preferring to talk about today's activities. An Exec's conversation concentrates on what needs to be done. They are not too keen on hypothetical discussions, which they often see as pointless arguments. They prefer to talk about people rather than ideas.

Execs have most difficulty communicating with Drivers. Drivers appear too impulsive – they speak quickly, think quickly, and move quickly, they don't give the Exec enough time.

Prepare your arguments in advance when dealing with Drivers. Talk about gains in efficiency, productivity, performance and effectiveness. Show how the 'bottom line' will be improved through savings or greater output. Don't get bogged down in the detail of doing the job. Stick to outlining your thoughts and the Driver will give you a quick decision.

Controller

Controllers are analytical thinkers, who like to examine the fine print for inconsistencies and flaws. They monitor the working of the team and are quick to criticise (not just for the sake of it), but don't like to be on the receiving end! But others may think that they talk too deliberately, concentrate too much on detail, are too cautious and too sensitive.

Controllers speak clearly, precisely and usually slowly. They are diplomatic and would rather seek clarification by asking questions than by making demands. They are not usually aggressive and may avoid conflict, especially of a personal nature, by walking away from it, leaving each party to go their own separate way.

While not outwardly aggressive, the Controller's ability to invest details, with apparently the same level of importance as a major decision, can provoke aggression and frustration in others. A Controller in a leadership position will often defer decisions, asking for more information and criticising the preparation of the material provided. For this reason you can often spot them in some companies, where they become known as the 'Abominable No-man'! They don't see themselves as blocking progress, merely applying the disciplines.

Controllers have most difficulty communicating with Enablers. They find them frivolous, flighty and lacking in perseverance. Controllers find Enablers too optimistic – why can't they see all that could go wrong? They see them as far too talkative – they don't give people a chance to explain everything!

When dealing with an Enabler remember that they like excitement! Talk about the challenge of the new goal, new strategy, or whatever else is new. They will not stay still long, so prepare in advance and state your requirements in short sharp sentences. But do try not to be dull! Expect to be interrupted – so keep track of where you have got to – and get back on course as soon as you can.

How to lift the communication mask

We have all known someone of whom somebody else has said: 'Oh they're all right, when you get to know them! Their bark is much worse than their bite.' In other words, their behaviour did not match the impression created by their words. They were projecting a role.

While it is a common occurrence for people to try and project the role they believe the occasion or the environment demands, few of us can produce the full effect by matching the behaviour as well as the words. The results are twofold:

1. If this an unconscious style shift, we may be misunderstood. Indeed, we may end up being assigned tasks which appear to match our communicated role and harvest an unwanted burden of stress as a result.

2. If this a conscious shift, we will be in danger of producing a parody of the role. Our body language may well display our discomfort and behavioural mismatch. Our speech patterns will display all the words but lack the tonality of the real thing. The effect will be seen on all around us: discomfort; at times increasing to the point of embarrassment.

The comments may well start:

■   'There's something funny about this guy, I can't quite put my finger on it.'

- 'Why does he have to do this? He's so good normally.'
- 'What does she think she's playing at? She's making herself look ridiculous.'

A typical example is the accountant who has been newly appointed as Managing Director to curb the so-called excesses of a Driver/ Enabler predecessor. Their most likely role will be Controller, but they may believe that, in the new appointment, people will expect them to be 'good on their feet'. So the important day arrives, perhaps they are going to address the sales conference or play host at a hospitality exercise.

Instead of backing off and letting the management team's Enabler (usually the sales director) handle it, they give their interpretation of the previous Managing Director's role. They either manage to sound like a hard sell double glazing salesman, or the words come out but the intonation and sincerity is lacking. If they are on the speaker's platform, they are not relaxed, but grip the lectern for dear life.

Conscious efforts to project a role can only be made to work by training and practice, for example a course in public speaking or presentation techniques can work wonders and will increase their role comfort if not their actual preference for the task. Of course, in time, they may grow into the role, but some people will be too set in their ways to make the change. It is far better to recognise one's role limitations, avoid the stress and let the appropriate team member pick up the task.

You may find it difficult to differentiate the communicated roles face-to-face. Is Frank a Driver, an Enabler or a warm and friendly, supportive Exec? At times, one characteristic can come to the fore and screen the real person underneath. Other than having a longer period to get to know the person concerned, what can you do? Try a paper diagnosis. Each role will come through, even if the face-to-face communication style masks the role behaviour. Look at the five memos on the same project below and jot down the role you believe they reflect:

Memo 1

XXXX Product Launch

The launch of XXXX is slipping behind schedule. The delivery of packaging to production was 17 days late, and some of the outer boxes were damp on arrival.

Some of you are not completing the 'received condition' box on the new 'goods received' note. We desperately need this information to ensure that incidents like the one above are responded to correctly and do not occur twice. We have 44 more working days to go to the launch. Make it happen!

Memo 2

XXXX Product Launch

Great news! Joe has got a launch stock commitment from Smith's. Who is going to be next?

The new packaging has now arrived and looks smashing. Note: some of the outers got damp in transit – they are fine for carrying sample stock in the back of the car. See Fred in the warehouse for a supply. Forty-four days to go! Things are really starting to *buzz* – don't forget the Launch Meeting on the 25th – see you there!

Memo 3

XXXX Product Launch

I'm sure you would all like to join with me in wishing Joe hearty congratulations on the order from Smiths. Well done!

The new packaging has finally arrived and will do much to improve the perception of the product and company quality. To make up the time lost I propose that extended shift working be employed until the 25th, by which time the national account forecast will have been achieved.

In 44 days we will be taking a major step forward for the company and its standing in the marketplace. Let us make sure we hit our targets and we will all see the impact on the profits and our future.

Memo 4

XXXX Product Launch

We will need to organise extended shift working from now until the 25th of this month. Please let Mr Jones know if you cannot be available due to personal commitments – I am sure we will cope somehow.

The new packaging is here at last. Please take great care with it until you are more familiar with the new filling procedure. The metric outers to go with it have also arrived. (Don't forget 50s now, not 48s.)

I am reminded that we have only 44 days to go until we shall see ourselves on television. I am sure we will all pull together and make every effort to get everything ready in time. Thank you.

Memo 5

XXXX Product Launch

We are now 44 days away from the television launch of XXXX, the first fruition of the new product development programme begun in 1990.

Post launch monitoring of the pull through by the TV advertising, backed by the product usage and satisfaction rating questionnaire to be included in the first 10,000 packs will provide us with an unprecedented level of information for a launch of this type into the Do-It-Yourself market sector.

The questionnaire leaflets will be arriving in four days' time for incorporation into the packs, which themselves have only just been received. Please let me know if this causes undue strain on the production schedule.

The roles: 1: Controller 2: Enabler 3: Driver 4: Exec 5: Planner

Lifting the mask is **not** something you should do to someone else. You will probably only embarrass them. It is something you should attempt to do for the rest of the team: *Lift your own mask* – if you are projecting a role, and be open with your fellow team members. The benefit in reduced team and personal stress will be well worth the effort.

5

Creating the Team

Whether a new team or existing team, the first step in creating a successful team is to create a complete team. It looks easy in theory: with new teams just make sure you have all the roles present; with existing teams change the people until you have a full set. If it was that simple, all teams would be teams of five, provided that all the specialist knowledge and skills were available. In practice we may have an existing team of three who own the business, or need to recruit a team of eight to meet the anticipated task load.

It may well turn out that the team of three has the potential to work as a complete team, while the team of eight can only raise three roles between the lot of them!

The issue of leadership will probably also have to be addressed. While there are some partnerships where the practise of leadership may even be irrelevant, most people when they consider putting a team together start by looking to appoint someone to lead or manage it.

LEADING THE TEAM

We have all felt at one time or another that, if only we had been in charge, this or that mistake would not have been made, or that the job could have been done better with a lot less hassle and reworking. So what if we were given the chance to affect the areas we knew best? To lead the team at those times when we were best suited and most sure of the ground.

Despite most people's assumptions to the contrary, it's *not* necessarily the Driver who leads. If it were, we would have called this role Leader instead of Driver.

The team is likely, when its task is finished, to have arrived at a destination first chosen by the Driver, but this isn't quite the same thing. It will, if you like, have been driven like a car, not like a herd of sheep. The Driver may have picked the area to go towards, but the Planner has navigated and identified the best route (with alternatives in case there are road works). The Enabler has filled its tank and polished it, the Exec has done the driving and stopped the kids squabbling in the back, and the Controller had all the insurance, licences and maps in order, while working out the fuel consumption.

If there is no team role of leader, who should lead? This will depend very largely on the job the team is trying to do. The question could be better put: If there is no team role of leader, how can you lead the team?

To achieve successful leadership in a team of equals there is an 'unlisted' role which needs to be adopted by all team members. To achieve maximum productivity and effectiveness requires all the contributions to be valued equally – but first you have to get everyone to make their contribution! To do this we use a leadership style that can be adopted by any role, that of:

THE MODERATOR

Leadership courses have stressed again and again that the leader must make the most of the variety of talents assembled in the team. In addition, each team member must feel that their contribution is *valued*. Praise from the leader (whether due or not) is not enough. Team members must feel within themselves that they have done well and given of their best. All top performing teams achieve this ideal.

The Moderator leadership style is the key that will unlock the suppressed potential of the team. This approach retains control and gives direction, but uses a minimum of instructions. It pulls the leader into the team and gets the contributions flowing. The aim is consensus – not enforced agreement! With role knowledge it becomes easy to ask the right questions and also know where to look for the appropriate contribution by role. Don't be tempted to run a one man band backed by a chorus of 'yes-men'. Once everyone feels that their contribution is actively sought and will be accepted, not jumped on, the recognition that each person can be different and equal begins to penetrate.

The Moderator can best be described as 'The Alternative Chairman'. It is an ideal style for leading team meetings in situations where the people attending are at varying levels of seniority, the role of meeting leader falls to a team member who would not normally chair a multi-disciplinary or multi-level meeting, or the meeting comprises a team of equals.

It encourages involvement and participation by everyone around the table, helps draw reluctant contributors into the meeting, in particular those who may be ill at ease, and promotes the equality of all team members. It helps to overcome the diffidence of those people who feel that it is not their place to run this meeting.

The aim of the Moderator is to make progress by achieving consensus. This consensus is founded on everyone understanding and accepting the need for all the elements of a team task to be considered and valuing the contributions of all concerned. This applies even between role opposites.

In reality, while the team may recognise the need for all the tasks to be addressed and for everyone to make a contribution and not just to sit there, human nature being what it is, the team may still be reluctant to put that understanding into practice. A leader's approach might be: 'Come on, you know we have got to do it', whereas the Moderator's style will be more towards: 'We all know it makes sense, how can we make it work for us?'

To adopt the style of the Moderator, the leader (and whomsoever he passes the baton to) should become an involved participant, not a detached circus ring master. They should try to sit among the group and use open body language: hands open with palms facing upward, arms moving freely at either side, body slightly leaning forward in a 'sending posture'. A typical example of these movements is demonstrated by any competent TV weatherman. They should not try to reflect the prestige of their position by making sermons from the pulpit or the head of the table, but make sure they are sitting in with the team. If someone has to sit in the power position at the head of the table, a Moderator would ask the person he or she most wants to make a real contribution to sit there. They should feel no need to defend their titular leadership with the symbols of authority: to sit with crossed arms or an artificial barrier such as a pile of paperwork, nor disguise their discomfort at the temporary transfer of control with flamboyant gestures, which draw all eyes towards them.

The effective Moderator will make regular eye contact to check understanding, consciously use body gestures (they may well become 'touchers' as they get used to it) to indicate reassurance, encourage a contribution, or acknowledge a point well made. They will prompt the team to analyse, evaluate and estimate, then summarise the key points before taking decisions, also using check questions, such as: 'Have we considered all the factors?', 'What have we learned?'

At all times they will seek solutions based upon consensus founded on common ground. The Moderator should show little interest in the status, relative power positions or importance of the players whatever their title outside the team context.

The last and most efficacious rule is to smile! A smile will do more to encourage contribution than all the protestations you can make! At the same time the rules governing effective meetings still apply:

- remember the aim(s);

- keep on course;

- keep it short and simple;

- record action commitments and decisions.

The Moderator needs to keep the meeting on course to achieve the team's aims and to bring people back on track when they wander off at a tangent. Yet they must always appear open to new thoughts and suggestions, so don't rush in and cut somebody off in full flow – the danger is that it may never restart when they actually have something germane to contribute. The Moderator should not feel the need to issue orders, instruct or remonstrate. Indeed, in the context of a team meeting it should be inappropriate to do so.

There should be no need to be confrontational or pressuring in tone, even if two Drivers are having a head to head battle with the team looking on. Try to focus attention on key concerns and get the others to realise where you are going rather than simply continue to force a point in the face of opposition. The language should concentrate on expressing 'we' not 'I'. The place for the 'I' statement is only when expressing a view that reflects your personal role, not to impose a direction upon the team. Try to use open questions (starting with 'where, what, when, why, how and who?) and use phrases that encourage contribution. The following may prove useful:

'Tell me...'
'What do we think is achievable?'

'Where are the major stumbling blocks?'
'What would it take?'
'Let's try to identify the priorities. What should come first?'
'Who do we need to convince?'
'What are we going to need?'
'Let's consider how we could tackle the task.'
'It seems our most logical start point is the figures.'

At every stage remember to acknowledge contribution. You are trying to get the team to expose their thoughts, not to suppress them. Try phrases such as:

'Is that the whole story?'
'That's interesting. Would X (pick by the relevant role) like to take it further?'
'Let's reflect on the aims'
'That's worth considering, let's leave it on the table ... would anyone like to pick up from what X has just said?'

Before making a decision, attempt to summarise. Introduce this phase with phrases like:

'The group appears to be saying ...'
'On the basis of X, Y and Z we appear to agree that we will ...'

At every stage try to employ a style and use language that is intended to engender team cohesion. It implies that together we can get a result – divided we will not achieve anything.

Who then should take on the role of the Moderator? Anyone can. The key question is 'when'?

Driver: When there is the need to review strategy or team goals, discuss the need for change, go for a decision, run a problem solving or ideas session.

Planner: When there is a need to guide the team to develop and understand a strategy, to estimate the feasibility of achieving a chosen objective or to prepare detailed schedules.

Enabler: When there is a need to promote acceptance of a new challenge or direction, to gain the resources needed by the team, to negotiate and to rekindle the team's enthusiasm.

Exec: When there is a need to co-ordinate the team's actions to ensure that the work is shared fairly, to determine the best procedures for completing a task and to work to reduce pressure and stress.

Controller: When there is a need to review how the team works, to record and report progress towards the team's goals. To handle quality issues in terms of both the team's work and the satisfaction with its output, to find out what went wrong and why.

A team under pressure needs sensitive handling – a strong leadership style will often only increase the stress. The Moderator acts on behalf of the team, just simply co-ordinating and keeping discussions on track. They start by encouraging open discussion, try to involve everyone present, acknowledge every contribution and lead the team towards a conclusion or decision by prompting responses, or posing questions. At the same time, they try to minimise conflict by accepting differing points of view as contributions to be taken into account.

All very laudable, you might say, but what do I really need to do that's different? You may even have used some of the phrases we suggest to get your team going. Your open questioning approach is admired by all! So what is the difference between conventional leadership and moderating? After all they both need to achieve the same objective.

Conventionally oriented leaders believe that it is their duty to get the team to do the things they, the leader, want done and act accordingly. They seek to impose their vision and their standards on the team. This is why the role of Driver is often assumed to be the natural role for a leader – the Developer and Director characteristics coming to the fore. The result will be a team distorted by the leader's role effects outlined in Chapter 8.

Of course, a degree of distortion is almost inevitable. That is why it is important to think about role preferences when appointing function managers. Yet, while the day-to-day running of a sales team will benefit from having an Enabler at the head who has a good rapport and understanding with those who share the role, there are always times when the broader view must be taken. Using the sales team as an example, there will be times when they have to plan and organise the sales conference, review service and support approaches, or even, for major project sales, actually 'team sell' together with personnel seconded from other parts of the company.

To illustrate the difference in approach, let's look at a conventional sales manager's conversation as he sets up a project sales team. For a start, it will probably not include everyone and might go something like this:

'Okay, the meeting is set for ten o'clock, Tuesday. There will be four of them and five of us. Now, we're going to have to manage this one, David!'

'You bet we will! I can just see what will happen if we let Keith from development run loose in there... he could say anything. And you know Peter, he's so enthusiastic about the 3150 and we can't risk selling them up to there, even though it's a better machine.'

'Well it's up to us to get the thing to run our way. Peter's not so bad. Now how much time will you need?'

'About 30 minutes to make the presentation. I'll keep it tight, so there shouldn't be too many questions.'

'We'd better give Harry a script of what we want him to say, or he'll tie the deal up in a mess of contract points instead of going for the order. I'll make sure he doesn't get in the way. Can you grip Peter and make sure he toes the line?'

Manipulative, dismissive, tunnel visionary, exclusive and possibly even dangerous! All in an attempt to manage a team to achieve a desirable outcome. They are fielding the additional bodies as bodies. They have to have them, to match the expectations of the customer's team, but they don't value them, because they don't share their own Enabler role view.

Trying to create a successful team in similar circumstances might go something like this:

'Okay, the meeting is set for ten o'clock, Tuesday. There will be four of them and five of us. Now, we're going to have to manage this! Let's put an agenda together round the table and identify the issues. Peter would you like to start us off?'

'Well, there is one issue I'd like to raise: I know we've been thinking of the 2150 for this job, but we're going to be phasing it out next year and you know what that does to the support costs. I've got the latest information here and I think we can show them that not only will the 3150 perform better, it will actually prove cheaper over two years and save them a bomb over five, as the cost of supporting the old technology goes up.'

'That's worth considering, let's leave it on the table ... would anyone like to pick up from what Peter has just said?'

Looks round the table. Spots that Keith is leaning forward and looking round to see if anyone else is going to speak. Puts a hand on David's arm to stop him leaping in and nods towards Keith.

'I'm not sure if it's relevant, but I had one of their technical staff asking about the new ISO standard – the 3150 will cope with that easily, but we'll be pushing it with a 2,000 series. Of course the Japanese machine already meets it.'

'That's interesting. David? Would you like to take it any further?'

'There's a lot to think about here. Has Harry anything he wants to raise before I put in my two cents worth?'

'Well I am a bit worried about the reliability clause in the contract, 99.5 per cent serviceability without a back-up seems to be asking a bit much – it's way over the industry standard. They have only got to get it wrong more than once and we could face a big penalty. Can anyone suggest how we can police this one? It would seem to be out of our control.'

'I hadn't spotted that. I just thought it was normal. It must be negotiable, their last installation has been nothing but trouble. That's probably what's on their minds.'

Checks heads around the table. Team are leaning back waiting for the leader's contribution.

'I've got some detail to go through, but we can put that under the heading of presentation. Let's try to identify the priorities. What should come first?'

Open, constructive, allowing the roles who normally get buried by a stream of Enabler verbiage to get words in, inviting and getting a valuable contribution. This team is not just following the vision of the leader, however talented he or she might be. After all, no one is omniscient!

Making the Moderator style work for you is an essential step towards creating a successful team – try and lock these key points into your mind:

- The aim is to make decisions based on true team consensus. No attempt should be made to impose judgments from the chair.

- Use gentle, open questions: 'How do you feel about..?', 'What's your first thought on ..?' to open up discussion.

- Everyone should be prompted to contribute *in role:* the Planner to estimate outcomes, the Exec or Controller to comment on systems, the Driver to propose solutions, the Enabler on how to gain necessary resources...

The leader is thus freed to concentrate on achieving the real contribution best fitted to each team member. Projects run to time, satisfaction from feeling valued and in doing a good job grows, the team are supportive. The leader also feels free to contribute in his or her own role, reducing stress and building on innate preferences and strengths. Less charismatic than striding along at the head of a group of followers – well… perhaps! But far more productive and successful.

A final thought on the leadership issue: it took Moses forty years to lead his people out of the wilderness and he never did get to the promised land. That's where the authoritarian leadership approach of issuing your orders engraved on tablets of stone from the top of the mountain could leave you!

BUILDING THE TEAM

When building the team, while we have to take into account the job they are there to tackle, the creation of a complete team must be the prime objective. Indeed, we would suggest that you create a complete team from the best qualified candidates and then pick the leader according to the nature of the work that the team is being assembled to carry out. To do this, we will have to look at both the primary and secondary roles, together with any strongly preferred characteristics. To see how this works in practice let's start on a green field site:

THE NEW TEAM

Putting together a new team needs to start with some thinking about the overall nature of the job they are to do. Competent people can tackle almost any task assigned to them with the right specialist support. But ignoring roles until you have put the team together is like trying to win at poker while playing a blind hand. Sometimes chance throws up a winner, but you may end up with three of a kind when what you needed was a run!

Rule 1: Throw the net as wide as feasibly possible.

Don't eliminate anyone who may have relevant knowledge and experience at this stage, even if you don't think they will be the best person for the job. You may have attended a meeting when a known cause of team friction sent along their number 2 to represent them and been amazed at how well everything went as a result. This may well have been because they provided a complementary role for the team, were more used to working co-operatively and accepting other people's points of view. So if the top candidate turns out to be a prima donna individualist and adds yet another Driver to the team it may well be more productive to go for 'second best'.

> **Rule 2**: Let everyone know that you are trying to create a team built of equals and get them to complete the questionnaire in Chapter 2.

By all means copy the questionnaire and results tables in Chapter 2 (we have suspended the copyright for that purpose) but if you really want to put together a real team of equals you will need to get everyone to read and study their role advice from this book at some stage. Then they will usually want to read further to find out about the other members of the team and you end up with a queue for the book – that is why we have made it an affordable paperback!

> **Rule 3**: Don't just look at the paperwork.

Spend some time talking over their results: Does their role and task orientation match? Did they come out as you expected, or is their communication style out of synch? How will they respond under pressure or the lack of it? What sort of teams have they worked in and how successful were they? Was it a good experience for them or could it have gone better?

Time spent at this stage will save you hours later on.

You can now select someone to bear the title of 'manager' or 'leader'. Even the most diligent Moderator will impose a degree of direction reflecting their role on the team, particularly when the pressure is on. It is usually by placing priority on those tasks the leader feels must be done so that he or she feels comfortable, that they may distort the team's performance. In order to determine the role most suited to lead the team you will have to look at the following factors:

Team type: project or specialist?

The first and most critical understanding is how the team will actually be working on a day-to-day basis. Will they need to be a true multi-disciplinary team all the time or only when issues secondary to the primary function of a specialist team are to be handled?

For a project team, the primary requirement is to find the best person to act as Moderator in the group, so that they can generate the full contribution from the team. In simple terms, we are looking for a leader for this team whose desire for success is greater than the desire for placing their personal stamp on all the team's actions. One who is confident enough to accept the lead of other roles as and when required to maximise all round team performance.

In a specialist team, it will help if the titular leader has a role which matches the majority of the tasks: Controllers are the natural choice for the financial or quality controller functions and, for once, the role and job titles match. They must try especially hard to think as a Moderator on those occasions which require a team approach instead of the more specialised line function tasks of every day work. This also means identifying a group within the function area which will contribute as a team. It may mean having to place equal weight on the contribution of someone who is not in the main line of the function's management hierarchy, but provides an essential balancing role for the team when broader issues must be addressed. A Controller can provide vital diagnostics and analysis to a team from an Enabler related function; an Enabler can gain valuable resources to ease the task for a Controller related project. Neither is likely to be held in high regard by the role opposites who are in charge of the function, until they recognise where to look for the contribution and see the benefits that thinking and working as a team of equals can bring.

Time span: short and fast or long and sustained?

Time pressure is one of the major causes of team stress. Different roles react to it in different ways. Placing a role which thrives in a rapidly moving short-term environment, in charge of a team who need to function patiently and consistently over the long term to get results often causes stress for all concerned as the leader tries to generate the activity rate and excitement that *they* prefer. Turn it the other way round, and put someone with a long term view in charge of a short-term dynamic project, and they may still be preparing to get started when another team would have finished! Each role is thus more suited to set the pace for its own preferred type of activity.

Driver: short to medium term

While the Driver's Developer characteristic may have a vision of a far future, the Director and Innovator characteristics tend to make sure that this is what it remains: a vision. This role thrives on change and challenge and is thus ideally suited to forcing through a short-term activity.

Medium term (1–2 years) can also be supported, provided there is plenty of decision making and problem solving to be done over the period and the goal is clear and challenging.

In the longer term, the preference for change will tend to distort the vision. The desire to affect the bottom line too quickly can result in strategies being set and abandoned according to the tactical needs of the near future. In part, it is the predominance of this role in the managing director's position in entrepreneurial businesses, without the moderation of a Planner as chairman, which results in the perceived weakness of British industry requiring too short a period to generate a return on new development.

Planner: medium to long term

The Planner, almost by definition, needs time to get started. They need to do all the research and analysis which provide a secure basis for their plans.

As a result, they are not the best people to take on activities with a time span of less than six months. Even if the plans are already prepared, this role will wish to review them and check their accuracy before proceeding and their attention to detail means that they can always find something which has been overlooked in the initial attempt.

Enabler: short term – the shorter the better

Enablers seem to have an incredible ability to get things done at high speed. To anyone else it may seem like a nice idea and worth thinking further about – to an Enabler as he or she delivers it two days later, it was an opportunity not to be missed.

This is both their strength and their weakness as a role type. Enablers need a continuous flow of the new to get excited about and to get others enthusiastic about. Put them on a long term and repetitive activity and they begin to drift. They certainly will lose their cutting edge.

On the other hand: set them the impossible deadline, send them out under-resourced to conquer the world in a fortnight, give them the new in whatever form and ask them to get it accepted and used and the Enabler is the key role.

The Exec: medium to long term – the longer the better

The hard slog, the sustained push, the objective that will only be reached by patient effort – that is the key to the time frame preferred by the Exec.

They like and need the stability of long term relationships. It is no hardship to them if the activity stretches before them without a defined end point.

Controller: medium if pushed, long term preferred

The Controller needs a past to analyse. While they may show those around them the lessons to be learned from a short-term project, they may delay one that is being run fast-track by insisting on sticking to the rules, especially if they made the rules in the first place!

The need to create a working structure to measure against makes the Controller more suited to those activities where the end result is finite, measurable and long term. They will be quite happy if the impact of their team's contribution is only perceived as a process of gradual improvement. It is then that their meticulous accuracy, record keeping and quality orientation will have time to be seen as positive benefits, rather than as a faultfinding drag on a team which needs to be finished by Tuesday – not next Christmas.

They may combine well with the Exec to sustain a continuous and disciplined effort over a long period.

Type of task: predominant nature of the work

Once the desirable role/time horizon is understood, the next factor to consider is the nature of the work to be done. Once again try and play to the preferences of the role:

Driver: The characteristics of this role lean towards new challenges. They will actively seek opportunities to be creative, solve problems, and break with the past. Drivers are the people to introduce change, as they consider that 'We've never done it that way', to be a positive advantage. While they are not the best people to use on a long-term development, they are the ideal 'log jam' breakers and 'quick fix' developers.

Planner: This role is forward looking, logical, detailed, and structured in approach. They are ideal for research oriented activities, combining information gathering and analysis skills with an ability to set down the way forward in terms that the rest of the team can use. When the requirement is for someone to apply a proven method to an activity which requires technical knowledge and a disciplined approach, the Planners are in their element.

Enabler: If the activity has a high requirement for working with people who interact with or are clients of the team – purchasing, sales, negotiating, training, communicating – the Enabler's characteristics ensure a positive response. Implementing change: communicating the need, raising everyone's enthusiasm, negotiating and compromising to a successful outcome, gaining resources to smooth the path – the value of Enabler will be seen by all.

Exec: The Exec's characteristics make them excel in two directions. They prefer to get the work done, so are the ideal choice for teams engaged in production oriented, routine or sustained development work. They also prefer the people-based tasks of a caring or supportive nature. The Exec is thus strong in personnel and administration functions, especially if consistent support is a vital ingredient for success, such as career counselling, the sales office and maintenance areas.

Controller: The Monitor, Auditor and Evaluator characteristics display a preference for work involving analytical or quality oriented activities, where detail and accuracy are of paramount importance.

Environment: background to the work

Every activity will take place against a background environment. There will be occasions when this environment will seem to dominate the real activity – as the saying goes 'It's difficult when you're up to your backside in alligators to remember that you are supposed to be draining the swamp!'

If this environment reinforces the role preference, all well and good. The Driver, for example, will cope well in an environment needing or ready for change, while the Exec will be less comfortable. Conversely in a stable and supportive environment, while the Exec may feel entirely at ease, the Driver will be restless and may prove disruptive.

Driver: Feels most at home in a high risk, challenging environment. They relish the startup projects or new developments, heading into unknown territory. They are also the ones to force through courses of action in an environment needing or ready for change, or to dig out a group that has become buried in its problems.

Planner: A calm, intellectual, theoretical environment will reinforce the role comfort of the Planner. In an environment which depends upon precision and self-discipline, and is formal and/or conservative in its ways, the Planner will show to advantage.

Enabler: All action, exciting, fast moving – this is the environment for the Enabler. They prefer a medium level of risk, but don't mind if this is due to the fact that the area may be under-resourced or undergoing change. In fact when things need a spark rather than a shove to get going the Enabler is the one to make it happen.

Exec: In a secure, social, supportive environment the Exec will flourish and be a positive help to maintaining this working environment. They will excel in a situation requiring co-ordination – looking after a bunch of individualists for example and keeping them working together, and in keeping things going, so are ideal for production and operational environments.

Controller: When more dynamic roles would be screaming with boredom and complaining of the lack of challenge, the Controller will provide an anchor. Low risk, formal, disciplined, procedurally oriented environments hold no fears for the Controller. Where systems or paper-based operations are the basis on which all else depends, rely on the Controller.

Knowledge or prior experience

Does the team require a vast body of knowledge to be effective, as in a team designing an aircraft wing, or must it depend largely on technique and adaptability, such as a new product launch group. Each role will show advantages when this requirement changes:

Driver: If you are facing the unknown, in many ways the Driver will be the most comfortable. They can start with zero knowledge, but get by with innovative problem solving techniques. They will take the time to acquire the knowledge to appear competent, but don't expect them to be totally *au fait* with all the detail. Medium knowledge and a strategic grasp of the principles are more the Driver's level.

Planner: This is the role to turn to when the requirement is for medium to high levels of knowledge of both the required disciplines and task area techniques. Planners are often found among the more formally trained, and rate highly in technical specialist areas.

Enabler: To land running from a standing start, even if they have only zero to medium levels of knowledge is a mission for the Enablers. If you need fast learning and good communication/ negotiation techniques to get by this will always be the role.

Exec: When you really need experience as much as knowledge to get the job done look for an Exec. They perform well when what is needed is a medium to high level of knowledge as to how the job has to be done, based on several years relevant experience, particularly in specialist areas. They are the role with the patience to acquire in depth experience in, what may to others seem, a limited area.

Controller: Medium to high knowledge levels with an emphasis on procedural approaches and recording techniques call for the Controller role. As in the case of the Planner, they will, preferably, be formally qualified in the job area.

The person who is given the functional title of 'leader' or 'manager' must always be prepared to pass the leader's baton to the role most suited to a task area. This is the way to achieve the best performance of that team at that task. All the factors above are designed to leave the 'leader' feeling as comfortable and in sympathy with the needs imposed by the nature of the team's tasks as possible – they should then feel free to ask others to step forward as the task orientation changes.

But what if your team is complete in terms of specialist input – these are the people you must use – but isn't complete as regards roles? You will then be in almost the same position as someone looking at an existing team.

THE EXISTING TEAM

Let's look at a hypothetical team with six members. In the ideal case, we'll have one member with a *primary preference* for each team role needed: a Driver, two Planners, one Enabler, one Exec and one Controller. All we have to do is think about working together effectively and developing as a team. But what if this isn't the case? We may have one (or more) primary roles missing. Perhaps it's the Enabler.

Missing roles

The first step in transforming the team is to fill the *missing roles*. A team without a Driver may be poor at problem solving and decision making; a team without a Planner may not budget well and schedule poorly. Without both roles setting strategy may be weak.

A team without an Enabler may be weak at communicating and negotiating; a team without an Exec may produce little in the way of output. Without both roles, management of resources may be poor.

The Controller provides the feedback by which the other roles manage – no Controller can mean quality is low.

You have three options to fill the role(s): Transfer, Spread and Recruit/Co-opt.

Transfer

Transfer is asking a team member who has a strong secondary preference for the missing role to consciously step forward and pick up the role for the team. By a strong secondary preference, we mean a role score greater than 30.

Transfer is the easiest solution to cover a missing role, especially if there is only one team member who shows it as their 'second choice'. If one member has a well balanced preference for the role, which scores close to their primary role, they may well be picking up the role for the team already. It will be a natural role shift for them. But what if there are two? Look at the score sheets below: who would you pick to fill the Enabler role for the team?

Both candidates have the same role score for Enabler. It would appear that the candidate on the left strongly prefers the Promoter aspects of the role, while the candidate on the right sees the Resource Manager's tasks as more attractive. Both have a 'weak' characteristic, a common feature in secondary roles, indeed the usual reason why the role qualifies as secondary. Don't worry about this – we are looking at preference not ability here. You will have to make your own judgment as to their ability to 'sell' and enthuse from the Promoter characteristic. In any case you can develop their comfort in the role by task based training (see Chapter 8). If this was their primary role choice there really wouldn't be anything much to choose between them.

However, we are seeking someone who can switch consciously to the Enabler role and comfortably maintain it for the team. To do

1 2 3 4 5 6 7 8 9 10 11 12 13 14 15		
A: DEVELOPER		14
B: DIRECTOR		14
C: INNOVATOR		13
DRIVER		41

1 2 3 4 5 6 7 8 9 10 11 12 13 14 15		
D: STRATEGIST		11
E: ESTIMATOR		4
F: SCHEDULER		4
PLANNER		19

1 2 3 4 5 6 7 8 9 10 11 12 13 14 15		
G: RESOURCE MANAGER		10
H: PROMOTER		14
I: NEGOTIATOR		9
ENABLER		33

1 2 3 4 5 6 7 8 9 10 11 12 13 14 15		
J: PRODUCER		5
K: COORDINATOR		8
L: MAINTAINER		12
EXEC		25

1 2 3 4 5 6 7 8 9 10 11 12 13 14 15		
M: AUDITOR		3
N: MONITOR		10
O: EVALUATOR		4
CONTROLLER		17

1 2 3 4 5 6 7 8 9 10 11 12 13 14 15		
A: DEVELOPER		12
B: DIRECTOR		7
C: INNOVATOR		12
DRIVER		31

1 2 3 4 5 6 7 8 9 10 11 12 13 14 15		
D: STRATEGIST		12
E: ESTIMATOR		11
F: SCHEDULER		12
PLANNER		35

1 2 3 4 5 6 7 8 9 10 11 12 13 14 15		
G: RESOURCE MANAGER		14
H: PROMOTER		9
I: NEGOTIATOR		10
ENABLER		33

1 2 3 4 5 6 7 8 9 10 11 12 13 14 15		
J: PRODUCER		5
K: COORDINATOR		7
L: MAINTAINER		8
EXEC		20

1 2 3 4 5 6 7 8 9 10 11 12 13 14 15		
M: AUDITOR		4
N: MONITOR		5
O: EVALUATOR		7
CONTROLLER		16

this it helps if the points difference between the primary and secondary roles is as small as possible – certainly less than 6 points. The right hand candidate shows only a two point difference. They may even be switching to Enabler for the team quite naturally. It's just that the Promoter characteristic by which most people spot an Enabler is not very pronounced and may lead you to think that the other candidate is a better choice – they may just like being on their feet!

In fact the candidate on the left shows signs of role polarisation and may not be very happy in sustaining their secondary role. Instead they exhibit a pattern we term 'Driver reinforcement': Strategist to get the team going their way, reinforced by Promoter to raise their enthusiasm, Maintainer to smooth out the people issues as quickly as possible and Monitor to keep an eye on them and circulate their version of the action plan! (Taking the minutes is part of the power game to someone like this.) This approach of dipping into role characteristics to fix problems can, in the short term, mask the unacceptable (to some roles) face of the Driver role, but it relies on speed to carry it through. It tends to leave behind comments like:

> He's done it to us again! Appears for ten minutes, picks on what we haven't done (Monitor), pushes aside the problems (Director), talks about future direction (Strategist) and fires everyone up (Promoter), grips a few elbows and says "Well done" (Maintainer) then vanishes again. Nothing has really changed. We're still in the mire, because we never get down to the detail.

The second candidate doesn't seem to know what they prefer to be – Driver, Planner and Enabler all within 6 points of each other. In fact this is a well balanced profile of a type displayed by those who are open and flexible in their approach: an ideal team player who will perform well at a wide range of tasks.

Remember: A team built of equals is about *preferences*, not about strengths and weaknesses or skills and ability. Don't confuse a high level of preference with a high level of ability!

So when looking for a candidate to pick up a role by transfer:

- Look for a secondary role score greater than 30 in the required role.

- Always prefer a candidate with less than 6 points between their primary and secondary role scores.

- Don't worry about an apparent role 'weakness' – if it's real, task based training should fix it.

But what if we don't have an obvious candidate and there is no one with the secondary role we seek? We must then move on to the next steps to cover the role(s): Spread or Recruit.

Spread

Role spread is a role sharing approach. It may appear an easy option, but is one of the hardest to implement well in practice. Role sharing is only easy when full role members attempt it.

Spreading requires two or three people to fill the role who have a strong preference for the required characteristics. To be successful, they *must* find the time to work and interact *together*. Problems will arise if they cannot link to produce a complete role: a Strategist who ignores an Estimator's feasibility study and a Scheduler who follows his own views on plan timings to the exclusion of both, will add little to team performance.

Chart the team's results to see who shows the strongest preference for each needed characteristic. Only put down the score if it is greater than ten (in other words, 11–15). If no one scores high enough to spread, leave the characteristic blank. While you are at it, why not log who on the team has the highest score for all the other characteristics? It will show how roles already filled might be shared to advantage.

A typical team might look something like this:

Role	Characteristic	Highest Found	Name
Driver	Developer	14	Arthur English
	Director	15	Peter Scotland
	Innovator	15	Arthur English
Planner	Strategist Estimator Scheduler	14	Peter Scotland
Enabler	Resource Manager	12	Arthur English
	Promoter	14	Arthur English
	Negotiator	12	Sarah Welsh
Exec	Producer	13	Sarah Welsh
	Coordinator	13	Sarah Welsh
	Maintainer	13	Sarah Welsh
Controller	Monitor Auditor Evaluator	12	Peter Scotland

Roles against which you cannot put a full set of names cannot be spread successfully. For this team, in order to fill the roles adequately you would have to recruit or co-opt a new team member.

There is little point in trying to compromise at this stage. You will just end up attempting to assign tasks to those for whom it's a chore and thus they have little inclination towards doing.

By now you should appreciate what will happen if a team member is given a list of six things to do for the team before the next meeting, which includes an out of role task. Five of them get done well and the sixth doesn't get done at all, or is done poorly. The reasons given for this may be plausible, but we now know what the real truth is: it's because the team member in question disliked or felt apprehensive about this particular task and did the other five first.

Once again, this has little to do with what the actual job may have been (the function needed to perform it) but rather with the way that jobs of this nature need to be approached. In other words, the role needed to perform it.

Case 4: The Programmer

It is often assumed that a computer programmer is an expert who knows all about computers. As a result, because he appeared to understand the technology a project team made a programmer responsible for choosing, ordering, chasing up, installing and maintaining the computers they all needed to use.

However, while programmers appear able to talk to computers, they often don't communicate too well with anyone else. Phrases such as 'He's only just on the planet' are often used to describe them. Programmers are only too likely to score somewhere around zero as Resource Managers. The result will be haphazard at best – in our experience, the better the programmer the less regard for good sourcing practices and budgets they exhibit.

The project team got into serious trouble by ignoring roles in areas where they thought things were too technical for the right team member to tackle. The idea of using the programmer to support the team's Enabler technically was foreign to their independent way of working. As a result they assigned the luckless computer programmer what turned out to be a complete project in its own right and left him entirely unsupported. As things started to slip, they unconsciously piled on the pressure, continually disrupting the programmer's work pattern, which resulted in him making mistakes and produced a crop of 'bugs' needing to be fixed, putting the main project even further behind. They only found out what was really going wrong when the programmer was discovered to be missing from work and was found sitting in the local park crying, totally defeated by the resultant stress.

Assigning tasks out of role does not just drag down team performance – it can damage individuals in severe cases.

Recruit

To use the team of equals approach to recruit or co-opt a new member to fill the missing role, follow the procedure outlined for assembling a new team earlier in this chapter.

Co-opting on a temporary basis, or even to attend specific meetings, may seem a more politically acceptable solution, especially in management teams. We have had several cases where a senior secretary or PA was co-opted to fill the vital Exec role in a Driver dominated team. In each case, the hardest part was to achieve equal status and acceptance of the contribution, despite an understanding of what they were attempting to do. Those teams who succeeded in integrating their co-opted member proved to be those who best adapted to the Moderator style and could bring themselves to let the baton go when the time came.

Those who failed brought career competition into the board-room and spent their time fighting their corner instead of looking to contribute to all areas of the business. They clearly believed that some should be more equal than others.

In our experience, it is better to bite the bullet from the beginning and accord equal status to a recruit to the team, or you will stifle their contribution. Don't look on it as 'diluting the team's status,' as one hide bound team member expressed it, but as preventative medicine against avoidable stress.

6

Causes of Team Stress and What to Do About It

Our work in developing the concepts which led to *Successful Team Building* has identified four potential sources of stress in team working. Two of these relate to the composition of the team; two to the individuals who make up the team:

- Natural Opposites: stress caused by inter-role conflict. eg, the clash between those whose natural instinct is to be an Enabler and those who prefer to be Controllers.

- Team Cohesion: stress caused by the make-up of the team – a team of teamworkers with the probability of low stress, or a team of rugged individualists.

- Role Shift: stress associated with the change of preferred role under pressure.

- Communication Mismatch: stress induced by a poor match between the enacted role and the communication style used.

WHAT SORT OF TEAM?

From the first two sources of *potential stress* it is clear that a certain level of stress potential is inevitable in any complete team. Yet some teams, even if they aren't very effective, seem able to avoid stress and all get on terribly well, while others, who certainly get the job done, seem to fight and argue most of the time.

When we looked at all the many different teams in detail, a pattern began to emerge. Our analysis showed that team role composition could be split into two basic types: Homogeneous Teams and Composite Teams.

THE HOMOGENEOUS TEAM – CLOSE HARMONY

First and most common, particularly in the professions and among groups who have gone through similar technical training, is a team which contains only one or two role types. In some cases the team will have literally eliminated anyone who did not match the dominant role type. In the recession of the 1990s, this tendency has become exaggerated as teams seek to dump those who don't conform to the team norm, often by making them redundant.

Case 5: The team of Drivers

A team of engineers had eased out everyone who didn't look to them like a Driver. As part of this process, they had made all the Execs redundant and discovered to their surprise that project timings had started to slip. Surely this dynamic, creative powerhouse they believed they had created should perform better, once all those people who kept getting bogged down in the day-to-day activities or buried in the detail, had been moved out of the way?

The only non-Driver to survive was the Planning Engineer, who communicated like a Driver! Needless to say, this particular lady was showing all the classic symptoms of stress from maintaining this role projection. As she told us: 'I'm not like that at home or away from work. It's just that if you don't talk like them, nobody around here takes any notice of what you say.'

Our team of Drivers all took rapid decisions on minimal data, problem solved when things went wrong, changed direction rapidly, took more decisions and so on and so on… Their low performance was due to the fact that they were all trying to get other people to produce the work for them, just as the Execs had done in the past, but there was no one who would step forward *consistently* to fill the role. Work was being done, but only when an imminent deadline forced someone to face up to the task. Work was either late or rushed.

The solution proved extremely difficult – they couldn't re-hire to fill the roles they needed, even though they now could see the value of those they had dismissed as plodding workhorses. That would have meant firing some of the 'good chaps' they had retained. Instead they went through a painful process of enforced role adoption, making as much use as possible of positive characteristics and role sharing whenever possible to support each other. Gradually they evolved six successful working team combinations from a department of 20 (some were in two or three teams) by being constantly on guard against their homogeneous team blind spots.

Case 6: The team of Planners

The Marketing Department of the UK operation of an American multi-national was a very pleasant place for a Planner to be. Over the years the head of department had gradually replaced his team with what he considered to be the right sort of people. Like him they were all graduates with blue chip marketing experience. As a team they looked impressive: the majority were tall, well groomed and sure of themselves. They knew they were there to guide the company towards a bright future.

The department's output was impressive – if you counted the number of words set down on paper. Individual marketing plans often ran to 25,000 words, the budget input to 50,000 and the strategic plan to almost 75,000. The theoretical quality of the work was impeccable.

The UK company was untypical of the worldwide operation. It was a well established business purchased by the US operation to spearhead its entry into Europe. The UK marketing was held up to others as an example to all.

Unfortunately, the company's new product and market initiatives always seemed to run out of steam. Products were late. Sales proved more difficult than anticipated. Competitors, particularly in mature markets, were price cutting aggressively to protect volume share. The marketing department reported all this dutifully and prepared more plans, using newer and even more advanced techniques. Often these ended up under resourced – the budget always seemed to get earmarked for other things.

Some of the members moved on – their career plans demanded it at this stage – but new recruits appeared, almost indistinguishable from those who had gone before. But of course they had a learning curve to go through. Then they had to review and assess the work of their predecessor and get up-to-date market information. It seemed that each product manager had only just got up to speed when it was time for them to go.

The UK Managing Director was destined for greater things – a fast track operator. While his marketeers were good political ammunition in the international company scene, market share was being eroded and sales volume was stagnant in real terms. He decided that the team was in need of a shake up.

A check of the role types within the team revealed a majority of Planners with the odd Exec and Controller in service functions.

The solution: an injection of market experienced Enablers were promoted in from the sales team. They needed a lot of help with the planning but they were tactically aware and capable of firing up the rest of the company to get the support resources mobilised. The Marketing Department head, to his horror, found himself reporting to a Driver/Enabler, the Sales Director, who took a direct hand in running key meetings. The Exec and the Controller were moved to report direct to the Sales Director and given increased responsibilities.

Gradually each side began to find out how to work with and accept the other's contribution (Planners and Enablers are role opposites (see below)). This took time and role counselling. For a while it seemed as if the marketing department would split into two warring camps, each derisory of the other's efforts. To broaden the base and gain a more balanced team approach, product line teams were introduced, combining marketing, sales, development and production. Care was taken to make sure these were complete teams. The place began to hum.

The tactical marketing budget suddenly became available as the Enablers went to work – they always seemed to be able to buy twice as well as the Planners – some of their deals were outrageous. The impact on sales was immediate. From a stagnant start, the company achieved 13 per cent real growth in a year.

The team of Planners weren't bad planners; they just couldn't overcome the performance handicap of being a homogeneous team.

Case 7: The team of Enablers

This team had been highly successful working together in their previous company. They had taken the best (in their view) of the sales team to which they belonged and set up on their own as distributors of an overseas competitor's products.

Sales started with a bang; the orders came flooding in. The management team were overjoyed. They had always known they could do it! To meet demand stocks were air freighted in. This pushed the overdraft facility to the limit and more warehouse space had to be hired. Then the problems started:

Technical problems – the competitor's products were subtly incompatible with those of the previous company – fixable, but it all took time.

Financial problems – customers didn't pay up until the technical problems were fixed. Some went back to the original supplier, others deferred the call off against their orders.

Staff problems: salesmen who were expecting and needed fat commission cheques weren't earning.

Administration problems: paperwork disciplines were ignored. The accounts were a mess. Stock records were inaccurate, as warehouse disciplines were ignored to meet the demands of the moment.

Everything they tried to do only seemed to make matters worse. The company's original supplier of funds included a venture capitalist. He could see that the team's enthusiasm was undiminished, everyone was working very hard, but the Managing Director was beginning to behave aggressively and get buried in the problems.

When we looked at the team, they were predominantly Enabler/Execs or Driver/Enablers. Under pressure from the Managing Director, one of the Enabler/Exec's had started to pick up Controller role tasks for the team, while the Managing Director himself was shifting to Planner. Both felt that they were becoming isolated from the rest of the team.

The solution: The Resource Manager characteristic of the Enabler helped to a degree, gaining sufficient additional funds to buy time. They didn't feel they could afford a full-time Controller, but were persuaded to co-opt a young accountant, who had recently set up in independent practice. They then looked round for a technical director who fitted the Planner profile.

Three years on they are still stretched financially but the company continues to show growth and has gained a fairly solid reputation. The team of Enablers were superb as Enablers, but the missing roles meant that many of the things they did to meet tactical needs only exacerbated the problems. It's no good running fast if you don't know where you are going and you can't see where you have been.

Case 8: The team of Execs

This team came into existence when the owner of a private company sold out his business after 20 years to a major oil company who were looking to diversify. In terms of turnover this business was pretty small in the parent corporate environment and, careful not to destroy their new acquisition by imposing a corporate structure more suited to a big company environment, they asked the owner for his advice in certain key appointments.

The owner had started life as a salesman and exhibited strong Driver/Enabler characteristics. He felt that all appointments should be made from within the company as a reward for loyal service. The only exception was to hire a Sales Director who effectively would be his replacement, while the former Technical Director would be made Managing Director.

The management team were all long serving employees who combined the Exec role with either Planner (Managing Director and Technical Director) or Controller (Production and Finance Directors). Into this mix came the new Sales Director designate – a Driver/Enabler. The designate qualifier reflected the new team's caution: they wanted to be sure this would be the right choice for them.

In theory, they had just replicated the successful formula which had built the business over the last 20 years. In practice, instead of the Driver/Enabler having the full power of decision as in the past, decision making lay in the hands of the one role which is least comfortable making them. The rest of the team soon regarded the Sales Director as if he were a corporate bull in their precious china shop!

Even though the sales team responded well and new product and market initiatives brought fresh growth in a mature market, the rest of the board began to operate as a separate team. They considered the Sales Director to be too abrasive, too willing to make changes for what seemed to them the sake of change. The crunch finally came when the Sales Director proposed tidying up the lines of reporting and creating a more relevant structure for the sales, marketing and development teams.

It was typical of the work ethic of a team of Execs that they all had too many people reporting to them directly – as many as nine managers in one case. The entire business was handled on a piecemeal basis; fragmentation rather than consolidation was the rule.

The rest of the board read the Sales Director's proposals and nothing was heard for six months. They then came back with their own proposals, which were in essence an attempt to pull the teeth of the Sales Director, who claimed constructive dismissal, accepted a settlement and resigned. The team settled back with a sigh of relief and appointed one of the development group managers as Sales Director. Everything seemed to be fine, but the impetus began to slip away. The sales team, who had felt they were an elite, began to leave. Growth targets were missed and the parent company decided to act. They knew where the problem probably lay, as they had profiled all the key personnel before confirming them in their appointments.

The solution: the Managing Director was asked to take on a group development responsibility. A Driver/Enabler was put in his place. The Production Director was asked to return to the position of plant manager and he thankfully accepted, while the Technical Director took on the role of Quality Manager with the task of implementing the BS5750 Quality Standard throughout the company. The team was reconstituted over a period and the company restructured along more normal lines.

The company still has its problems, but they have not had to waste the knowledge and experience of the long serving employees the former owner wished to protect. Asking a team of Execs to take over from an autocratic leader put them in an unsupportable position, where the Execs' normal response of getting their heads down and working harder was not the answer.

Case 9: The team of Controllers

The Swiss-based President of a US corporation's chemicals division decided to implement a European management structure which reduced the autonomy of all the operating companies. After six months of this the UK company's Managing Director resigned.

The President appointed as Managing Director an Englishman from his European management team, who he held in high regard. His ability to work in the same way as the President and manage his group at long range just from the reports was particularly impressive. The new Managing Director was a Controller.

He succeeded a blunt Northerner with a good grasp of the realities of the market who was known and liked on the shop floor, where he got much of his information at first hand. Rather than hold meetings, he'd just let it be known that he expected key managers to turn up early for lunch in the boardroom.

The new Managing Director found all this incredibly amateurish and sloppy. For a while he attempted to maintain the culture, but his attempts were all out of role activities: he was too stiff and ill at ease to walk about the factory on his own and talk to people he didn't know, so he soon acquired an entourage for these visits and as a result he learned nothing. The informal nature of the lunches did not fit his corporate style. He had the canteen redecorated and then scrapped the boardroom lunches.

The reporting standards of his team of directors left much to be desired and over a period of two years he replaced them all with the exception of the Development Director who was also a Controller. The new Finance Director, Production Director and Personnel Director were all Controllers. They cleared the top floor of the office block, which had also accommodated one of the largest company divisions and settled down, each in their own office to run the business. The only member of the team not to fit the role was the newly appointed Sales Director, who matched the stereotyped view of an Enabler to the point of caricature, even down to his matching tie and handkerchief and fund of funny stories.

Every fortnight on a Tuesday the sales management team reported to the Managing Director's office to discuss their report and to be castigated for some new dereliction of duty. The sales teams went to great effort to put things right; on one occasion bribing every hardware store and garage in the High Street of the Managing Director's home town to stock a new display. (It didn't work – he found a shop ten miles away that they'd missed!)

The stories from all the affected middle managers were becoming apocryphal. The Sales Director developed a bad back which always seemed to cause him to miss crucial meetings – a classical sign of stress. Paperwork and control systems proliferated: nothing could move without at least two signatures. The entire board began to spend its time on planning a new computerised production control system. Thirteen organisation and methods staff were employed to look at 93 direct labour workers. The data processing department grew to five per cent of the company's employees as more and more reports were required.

Almost in self-defence, the middle managers began to form their own team: sales marketing, personnel and production developed an effective working group. They held their own meetings and took their own decisions. The team of Controllers certainly wouldn't make any – there never seemed to be enough information on which to make one, or it was badly presented and was sent back for rewriting.

The company nearly ground to a halt. The board proved that whole sectors of the business were unprofitable and closed them. The overheads couldn't be supported and staff were cut. In three years they took a profitable £16 million business and turned it into an unprofitable £14 million business.

The solution: The new Directors all began to abandon ship one by one. Even the Managing Director managed to move back to a group position. The parent group became alarmed and eventually an Enabler was appointed Managing Director. Backed by sound role based advice, he put together a small, but complete team. The company has taken years to recover from this excess of Controllers. They, in themselves, were all competent, qualified and experienced people, most of whom went on to do a good job in more balanced teams. They were only a disaster when working together as a homogeneous team.

You can liken the output produced by a homogeneous team to close harmony – they all sing around the same note but the sound is a bit lightweight – all tenors rather than a range from bass to soprano. Of course this team can be a very pleasant place to be. There is little role conflict – just like minds working together. It really all depends where the hole is. Some of them manage to drift along for years, but eventually the need for change or a crisis, often self-induced, will sink this unbalanced team.

THE COMPOSITE TEAM – TRUE HARMONY

Now take the other team type: combining all or most of the roles, with the full tonal value of true harmony, generated by a range of voices, enriched musically by the part singing counterpoint of argument and lively discussion.

It certainly takes time for this team type to achieve a balance and for all the voices to be heard. There may well be a degree of stress caused by the natural conflict between opposing views of the best way to work. Those whose careful attention to detail may slow the running rate of the fast track role types (who consider it nit-picking), may find the intuitive creativity of the others unsettling to their more measured approach (which in turn provokes the response that they can't seem to follow the same direction for two days running).

It is, however, a productive mix. Issues are less likely to be ignored. Decisions can be made on a sound and adequately detailed basis. Plans will be estimated and scheduled properly. Necessary resources gained, work done and quality checked.

Once this team type has an understanding of the roles which make up a successful team, they can begin to allow for the points of friction and respond by accepting the positive elements of their opposites' contribution, instead of dismissing it out of hand. The potential for stress will not go away, but it can be managed. As a member of one of our early teams said to us: 'I still don't like what X does, but I'm beginning to see the need for it and that makes it easier to accept.'

THE NATURAL OPPOSITES

Though capable of performing many roles, people usually have a preference for one or two at most and each role has its opposite in behaviour and style.

They need each other to perform effectively, but they do not attract! It doesn't matter that the communication is sound and the behaviour effective; the irritation caused can lead to conflict and this will cause stress. Because the combatants see their opponents differently – Execs see Drivers as arrogant and rude, Drivers see Execs as foot draggers – quick resolution is unlikely!

Understanding that this is happening is the starting point from which to work to overcome this stress, by recognising the differences that stem from preferred roles. The list below shows where conflict is likely to occur based on roles opposites.

Driver	The Exec
Planner	Enabler
Enabler	Planner and Controller
The Exec	Driver
Controller	Enabler

Drivers tend to see the Execs (with their steadiness and head down, get the work done attitudes) as unimaginative plodders, mere cannon-fodder in the battles of corporate life and thus expendable.

Planners see the Enablers (with their flexibility and communication skills) as flashy, fast talkers who trample all over their carefully thought out plans to meet the tactical needs of the moment.

Enablers find Planners and Controllers (with their careful analysis and attention to detail) as demotivating fusspots who always look on the negative side of any opportunity.

Execs see Drivers (with their willingness to accept change and rapid decision making) as disruptive power grabbers who ride roughshod over everyone else on the team.

Controllers see Enablers (who gain necessary resources for the team and negotiate well) as fly-by-night butterflies who will take anything they can find as long as its not nailed down and then give away something vital.

Guard against these reactions! They are difficult to eliminate because they each contain an element of truth and are not simply based on prejudice. Start by making a list of the role opposites in your team. The team's role opposite results can represent either:

- Good news – The list seems rather long and the potential for stress will be higher, *but* you now know what to watch for and you will have a more rounded team. A complete team should demonstrate a full listing of role conflicts when mature.

Remember to watch for an increase in friction if members are asked to try to step forward in their secondary role and help round out the team.

■ Bad news – There is little or no conflict in your team. This means a low stress potential from role conflict, *but* it also means that your team is incomplete. Teams with few role opposites are like that close harmony group: in result terms they are lightweight. To achieve the power of full harmony requires the full range of voices of a complete team.

INDIVIDUALS v TEAM PLAYERS – TEAM COHESION

Stress will occur when there is not enough cohesive force to keep the team moving towards its goals. Energy has to be spent keeping the individuals working together. Perhaps only the leader will feel the stress, but genuine teamworkers in the group will also suffer from having to field the internal problems – especially if time is tight.

Try to make the team attractive to its members to achieve cohesion. Attractiveness can be delivered in several ways.

Role sharing – like minds, working together; acceptance of common goals; good role fit and interaction; leadership and involvement in decision making.

It should be seen as a privilege to be part of your team. It also helps if the leader is team centred rather than leader centred! Team success should be your prime source of satisfaction. Seeking personal recognition at the expense of team performance destroys team cohesion. The other major factor affecting team cohesion is previous team experience.

Team Experience – the 'X' Factor

Even when you are all being open and honest with each other, working to reduce each other's stress, beginning to feel secure in your role and to acknowledge the value of the other roles on the team, there may still be those who seem to find difficulty working together.

As in all the aspects of the work which went to create the team of equals approach, we found that getting to know what to expect from each other in the future had not, of course, wiped the slate clean of all prior experiences. Even someone joining a team straight from school will have had good or bad experiences of team working which will more or less condition their response and contribution to the needs of a new team.

Some people naturally enjoy teamwork, others don't. They may be individualists by nature; but often it is their previous experience of team working which has led them to believe that the fastest way to get *nothing* done is to let somebody else in on the act.

We now know why this can happen. If you've worked in a team without a Planner, for instance, you will have discovered that if you know where you're going, but nobody's figured out how to get there and you may go round in circles or keep getting stuck in the same place. Your (incorrect) conclusion may be that 'Down to Gehenna, or up to the Throne, He travels the fastest who travels alone' (Kipling, *The Winners*).

A team, whose members are all highly cynical about the benefits of teamwork before they start, is clearly facing an uphill run. If it fails, we have a double disaster, since everybody becomes still more cynical. So it's a good idea at least to talk things over and see just how many cynics you have.

Team experience is the 'X' factor. It can be the hidden agenda, which reduces the effectiveness of an otherwise complete team. Every team member carries around memories of past team experiences, which colour their attitudes to team working. They may be natural loners, or those who claim to enjoy team working, yet carry a burden of frustration and resistance into each new team situation.

The only solution is to bring this hidden agenda out into the open. It doesn't matter if Sheila prefers to work totally independently and Joe seems to need someone holding his hand every minute of the day. They merely reflect different ends of the team experience spectrum. Some team tasks need a high level of independence: a resource manager who won't move on her own will acquire little for the team. Others require an ability to work together in harmony: a Maintainer who doesn't believe he should work with the others to keep the team functioning smoothly won't do much maintaining.

The spectrum of team dependence versus independence varies from high to low. Think back to your past team experiences: Were they good, bad or just indifferent? Can you identify and eliminate the role effects?

Ask each team member to attempt an honest self assessment of his or her position: How many would rate themselves as team players, based on past experience and how many incline towards independence? Read the advice spectrum which follows. Where would you place yourself?

Team player: It's the only effective way to work.

Almost too good to be true, this displays an uncritical support for teamwork. As far as you are concerned, if you had the choice, you would always be part of a team. Be on your guard – don't let the team end up carrying you as you lie back basking in the warm glow of team support and enjoy it!

You certainly prefer working in a team. The social contacts, the potential for increased productivity, the sharing of goals, the similarity of attitude between you and other people who like to be team members, leads to a feeling of contentment and security. There is a danger that this feeling – often felt by team members, because they rely on each other – may lead you to neglect the additional effort needed to keep the team active and growing.

Watch out! Don't keep your head down, look out for problems. Join in the problem solving and make sure that solutions are actually implemented. This will increase your contribution and value to any team.

Anchor: You take a positive attitude towards team working.

You can accept the necessary compromises for the sake of harmony and encourage others to do the same. You believe you are a good teamworker and this must be good for the team, and good for you. Your attitude to teams is both positive and realistic. You will tend to set your own goals, usually in harmony with the team, and devise your own work patterns to achieve them.

Try and be an anchor for the rest of the team. You will have had satisfying team experiences in the past and enjoy contributing, but can still question the team's relevance to a task.

Keep your eyes open for team problems. In particular, listen to the words of any member who appears not to wish to belong. These independents can often act as a mirror to the team and let you see yourself as others see you.

Average: Mixed feelings.

Like the curate's egg, your previous experience has been good in parts. You appear to be open-minded about the benefits of teamwork and your involvement in it. You can be unbiased when it comes to judging the relevance of team work to a given situation. If asked, you seem happy to join in, if not, you probably would not worry too much. Don't let this slip into indifference!

It is usual to consider teams as a group of people working together in a room, or playing together on the field. However, most of the team's work is done by people who have agreed the team's goal, accepted some of the tasks needed to achieve it, and then get on with the job. When you do disperse to work, be careful not to lose sight of your role as a team member.

Cautious: You have had your fingers burned in the past.

You may appear inclined to treat teamwork, if not with outright distrust, with at least a high degree of scepticism. To be involved with a team, or to take part in their activities, you need a well thought out justification.

This is in itself no bad thing, but it might mean that, unless there is a good Promoter amongst the other team members, you hold back from sharing your knowledge. This can't be good for the team.

You don't need to abandon this apparent preference for single-minded specialisation to be very valuable in the team's problem solving activities. Join in brainstorming sessions. Help them with data gathering and interpretation. You could both benefit!

Independent: You see yourself as a rugged individualist!

You may even deliberately take the position that you don't really want to play. It's quite a common profile in top flight sales teams, where the competition for top salesman is such that there are those who won't let themselves be distracted by the time demands of a team task which adds nothing towards their personal performance targets. (In part this shows why top salesmen often make very bad sales managers – they are not team minded.)

You are certainly more independent than the average team worker! You probably don't need what, to some, are the benefits of being part of a team. However, when you find yourself in a team situation, look for a positive role – even if it's only to break the team of their bad habits.

Though you may not wish to belong in the interdependent world of the team, you can still contribute to its effectiveness. There are tasks that you can perform that rely on your independence, and which are of great value to the team. Take on the jobs which need a great deal of self-reliance or are away from the team base environment, then show the world what you can do. You may come to enjoy the appreciation of the rest of the team!

Take another look around you: what sort of team experiences have coloured the attitudes of the other members of the team? Are they independent or team minded? They may have had good or bad experiences of team working in the past. Don't assume that their attitudes will be the same as your own, or you may just end up with a team paying lip service to your enthusiasm for teamwork. After all, expressing dissatisfaction with teamwork implies rejection of the other team members, unless you make it plain that you are interested in *past* experience as a basis for determining a better approach for the future.

Thus, if you are all going to work at creating a real team built of equals, share the problems you have had in the past with the rest of the team. This is often a good point at which to start discussing the effects of different roles on the team, based on what went right (or more usually what went wrong) and to begin to plan your way forward, trying to avoid making the same mistakes again. When filling a team, you ignore team experience at your peril.

Depending on the overall mix within your team, you will have one of three team types. If everyone on your team rates themselves as *team players* or *anchors*, you have a *team players* team. If *cautious* or *independent*, an *independent* team. If a mixture of both, a team with *mixed feelings*. Look at the advice which follows. If you can't make up your mind about the level of independence in your team by looking at the players, try and decide which advice seems most appropriate to your team situation.

A Team Players Team

This team appears on the whole to have enjoyed previous team experiences and understand and accept the value of working together as a team. There is only one failing to guard against – *complacency*.

- Don't let the desire to work closely together slip into 'hand holding' activities. You know each member's role, make sure they play them.

- Don't let the team get so comfortable they confuse 'happy' with 'efficient'.

- Remind the team constantly that to progress they must grasp new opportunities and that this will entail change. A complacent team won't rise to the challenges.

Mixed Feelings

This team's profile suggests only an 'average' attitude to teamwork. This may seem acceptable, but, to achieve this rating, your team must contain those who do not have a high regard for team working. The main barrier to good team working in this type of team is probably *indifference*.

- Who never has time to complete tasks for the team? Get public commitment to timings and set joint tasks when possible, so that working together becomes a team habit.

- Use members' individual skills to develop creative and shared problem solving projects.

- Get the whole team to input and commit to decisions. Don't take silence to mean agreement.

Independent

If a high degree of interdependent team work is necessary, you may have trouble. Many of this team's members seem to believe that teams are a luxury in which they need not indulge! Balance their desire for *independence* against the needs of the team.

- Check that a team is necessary in more than name. Must people work well together to achieve results? Are tasks highly interdependent?

- Play a major co-ordination role. Make sure independent contributions are directed at the team's goals.

- Get everyone to make a contribution to a decision and get commitment from individuals to carry it through.

HOW DO THEY BEHAVE?

Now that you have assessed the implications raised by the

structure of the team it is time to assess the stress potential created by individuals. The two elements are the effects of role shifts and of role/communication style mismatch.

Role Shifts

We have never seen a team in which role shifts did not occur under pressure. The effects can be positive, as someone steps forward to fill a role and complete the team, or and regrettably more commonly, negative as the role shift may homogenise the team or indicate the onset of a stress reaction.

Pressure response is not an absolute. Some people never seem to feel it, even though all around are running around like headless chickens totally stressed out! (This must have been the person Kipling had in mind when he wrote: 'If you can keep your head when all around you are losing theirs and blaming it on you'.) The secret is to develop good coping techniques.

Team based coping techniques start with openness: if the others aren't aware that you are feeling the pressure, how are they to know when to support you? Of course, you may blow your top or behave irrationally enough for the others to spot your problem, but by then you are usually already deep in the mire.

In a team built of equals you should feel free to express your feelings. There is even a role member who will help: the Exec, through the counselling nature of the Maintainer characteristic. Needless to say, our advice to an Exec who feels that they are under pressure is to let the others know at once! But just in case their natural reserve still inhibits certain team members, what should you look for?

Natural Shifts

Some team members display a natural role shift to their secondary preference under pressure. They may be comfortable with this, but you should watch for:

- Stress symptoms: increased tension, marked behaviour change (eg withdrawal by a member, unusual silence, lateness, or even absenteeism), sudden antagonism.

- Spontaneous role shift by a team member at a perceived increase in pressure (+ a domino effect of role shifts as other members move to accommodate the change).

Ask the team: What was the trigger? Is the change positive for the team? If not you must intervene and get everyone to step back and review causes.

Unnatural Shifts

Some team members move to a role other than their secondary role – this is an *unnatural role shift*. They may be perfectly capable of taking on the role, but are unlikely to sustain it, as it is not their choice.

- Stress symptoms: continuous task shifting, but little output – 'busy, busy'. Displacement activity – interfering in other role's tasks.

Review roles and task assignments with the individuals concerned. Help them to examine their motives for the shift and to reach a decision on the tasks to be tackled. Make sure that any tasks within this role are seen as temporary and encourage them continuously in order to achieve successful completion.

Role and communication style mismatch

Communication styles are the image we project to the world. We may wish to be seen as dynamic and thrusting, or thoughtful and caring – this will be reflected in our role preferences.

However, the way others see us depends to a large degree on the way we communicate. If this communication style matches our preferred roles, everyone knows what to expect. *But* if we say one thing and do another, we create discomfort or even stress among those around us.

Hopefully, most of the team will display a match between role preference and communication style. How then can you identify the potential problems caused by those in the team who seem to say one thing while doing another?

We have all let first impressions lead us to a wrong conclusion about someone. This shock may cause stress the first time it is encountered, but if the mismatch is constant, we get used to it. However, if there is an irregular shifting between roles and communication styles that don't match, it generates the pressure of not knowing what 'mood' to expect. Remember that we all put pressure on others. Role/Communication Style mismatch causes others to suffer.

Since the attitudes and behaviour of the Primary Role still come out, this mismatch causes stress – much of it in other team members – as they try to interpret the words in terms of the role they perceive. So watch out for the effect they are having on the rest of the team. Are others displaying discomfort? The symptoms are restlessness, looking away from the speaker, even provoking an uncharacteristically aggressive response.

It is often the case that these members believe they are being reasonable and clear, but get frustrated when misunderstood, as their manner acts to mask their good intentions. They may attempt to match an unnatural role and communication style: this may cause personal stress as it involves sustaining a continuous act.

Encourage the team to adopt an open style with each other and share their thoughts. Watch for signs of frustration in all the team's members and try to draw out the real meaning by gentle questions.

TOTAL STRESS RISK

So how great is the risk for potential stress in your team? Try the following check and see how you score. If in doubt, pick the mid point.

1. Count the number of role opposites in your team. Add 1 point for each individual in a pair.

2. Rate each member of your team for individualism – one point for Team Players, two points for Anchors, three points for Average, four points for Cautious and five points if they are definitely Independent by nature.

3. How many people make a role shift under pressure? Count 1 point if they don't change, three if it's a natural shift, five if you believe this to be an unnatural shift.

4. How many are there in the team who don't communicate in a way which matches their role preference, or whose role preference genuinely surprised you? One point if they match, three if they only slip away occasionally, five points for each person still wearing the mask.

5. Divide by the number of members in the team.

The three advice sections below each relate to a score band:
Over 11, 5–11, less than 5.

Over 11 – Team at Risk

The total stress acknowledged by this team gives cause for concern. Some pressure is needed for optimum performance, but not at this level. You should act now. Identify the major sources of pressure, and reduce them.

- Try to make the atmosphere as informal as the team culture will allow, but stay professional.

- Make sure everyone knows how the team is progressing, spend time on listening and work at openness.

- Watch for signs of conflict between members and be prepared to step between and moderate.

- Remember that poor meetings are a major source of stress. Prepare well and keep discussions on track.

Counselling individuals

You will have some individuals at risk from pressure. You may suspect that they are suffering from stress, *but*, you cannot just walk up to them and say: 'You are suffering from stress, how terrible!'

Make your initial contact a combination of observation and open questions. For example, if you see a person looking depressed, just staring into space, you could open the conversation by saying: 'You look a bit down in the mouth this morning. What's the trouble?'

The individual may not have acknowledged that there is stress, so don't use the word. Make it clear to the individual that you have noticed a change. Be careful not to make it sound like a reprimand. Make it clear that you are willing to listen.

Explore the problem. Help them to talk through the situation separating symptoms from causes. You may need to probe the real meaning of some of the statements and ask open questions to keep things going. You might try getting the person to draw a map of the problem, the input to it and the results arising from it. Identify the root causes – they may not be the same as the problem first expressed.

You can then look at the changes that need to be made to ease the pressure. You may need to help him or her discover self-induced pressure by encouraging them to talk about self-imposed standards: Are they the sort of person who strives for perfection in all things? Do they feel the need to get everything done yesterday? Do they have to do everything themselves?

Encourage them to be open in discussing things you could change in your behaviour or the organisation. Be prepared to accept criticism and, if valid, take the responsibility for improving matters. Commit with the individual to making the changes that will reduce pressure. This may include: providing information, reducing role/task overload, improving role/task integration, developing role comfort and performance through task oriented training.

Seek agreement from the individual as to the best way to achieve any changes for them. It's a good idea to lay out a change programme at this time, but, whatever you do, get going! You may think this will fix the problem, but you won't know unless you take the time to talk over progress at a later date. If there is a time critical element in your change programme, diary it and make sure you hold the conversation.

To summarise, the three key steps are:

1. Use discussion of how they feel about their team role to explore the problem and try to separate symptoms from causes.

2. Encourage openness, accept criticism and, if valid, act to ease the pressure. Pressure is often self-induced. Do self-imposed standards add to the problem?

3. Commit to making changes to reduce pressure. Agree an individual approach and get going. Meet regularly to discuss progress.

5–11 Build on...

This is a team that does not show a high level of stress. This does not mean that you can sit back and watch the world go by! You must keep them fit:

■ Make sure that all 'sensitive' issues are dealt with as they arise.

■ Keep some of your time free to stand back and observe the way the team is performing.

■ Discuss roles and work at role development. Who needs help with their role weakness?

■ Encourage openness: When a team member stops talking the problems can follow.

Less than 5. Oh Dear!

This team really get on well, but how much do they really produce? To score this low you must have a fairly homogeneous team and this may be reinforced by members who are so secure in their roles they are polarised (ie the secondary role score is less than 30 points).

■ Leaven the mix by introducing members to fill the missing roles.

■ Encourage the appropriate team members to develop their secondary roles for the team.

■ Look for someone to tackle those tasks which require independent operation.

■ Watch for the signs of complacency.

■ Watch for those who appear to have a hidden agenda and rely on other team members with the same role to make their contribution.

7

Making it Work: Team Working

Now comes the hard part – making it work for you and your team. A successful team will not spring into being fully formed just because everyone has read this book and is willing to give it a try. It will take careful planning and patient application of what has been learned so far. To achieve a fully functioning team we will have to do three things:

1.   Meet as a team.

2.   Develop as a team.

3.   Work with each other.

Simple phrases, but you will appreciate by now that everything about the concepts underlying *Successful Team Building* is simple. It is the practice that requires the thought, preparation and change of approach.

MEETING AS A TEAM

To meet as a team, instead of as a committee which reviews progress, will require several changes. Not just the change in the way you will all look at each other. As one member, who was surprised at the immediacy of the effect on the team which came from understanding their preferred team role, put it to us: 'No team which has gone through this process will ever look at each other in quite the same way again.'

To reap the benefits of this new viewpoint you will need to change the way you put together a meeting agenda. In addition, the meeting at which you all first come together as a team, sharing a common viewpoint, is a vital starting point and needs careful planning.

After everyone has completed their *Successful Team Building* self analysis questionnaire and read the role descriptions which apply both to them and to those around them in the team, the first team meeting can end up dominated by role discussion but inconclusive in terms of agreed actions. The main objective must be to get everyone to accept and use what they have learned and then to decide what each person is going to do to make the team work better. To achieve this you will need to prepare thoroughly.

Take the time to talk with all the other team members about their results before the meeting to discuss their role preferences (and, perhaps, the way they have always appeared to you). Then talk over their previous team experiences and get them to rate themselves for independence v team player. Then you should be able to put what you have learned together to build up an indication of the stress potential for the team.

If you are all coming together for the first time as a new team, it is even more important to take this time to learn about the rest of the team. Once you have had a discussion of this nature you should feel fairly comfortable with each of the people concerned and know how they feel about the approach and their results – the ice will have been broken, so to speak. Of course, this level of discussion may not be practicable due to time and/or location constraints, but in any event, even if you have all worked together for years, don't let apparent familiarity breed overconfidence: prepare in the same depth whether you have had time to talk to them all before the meeting or not.

Start by drawing up a team profile. To see how it is done, let us look again at the team used in the example in Chapter 5. As it is unlikely that in the real world you would be working blind, not having met the rest of the team, here is a thumbnail sketch of the three team members who make up our team example:

Arthur English: In his forties, moves quickly, talks quickly and is always coming up with ideas which approach problems from a tangential direction. Does not suffer fools gladly and can be abrasive. Career history includes ten year periods in both sales and marketing. A born optimist, prepared to tackle anything, but not noted for a long attention span.

Sarah Welsh: In her twenties, a graduate, a bright fluent talker who makes friends easily and keeps them. Has produced some very solid work on previous projects, often ending up carrying those around her. Is always sympathetic and willing to listen, when you can get a word in! Tries to ensure that everyone does their fair share of the work, relying on her enthusiasm to get everyone going when the pressure is on. Not afraid to take decisions, although occasionally goes off and works on her personal priorities as a result.

Peter Scotland: Early fifties, slow moving, smiling, slow talker. His writing style shows a predilection for precise wording which results in his communications being hard work or even obscure to read – over intellectualised to a degree. When pressed can erupt and will persist with his own perception of an issue, to the point of annoyance and beyond, in those around him. Very concerned with quality issues, which he will analyse in immense detail.

Now look at each individual's results because we need to know more about how this team will work together and to draw up their team profile:

Arthur English

Sarah Welsh

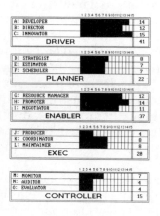

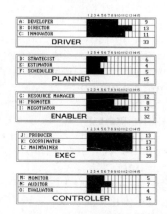

Peter Scotland

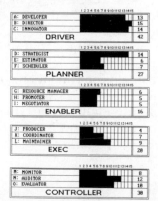

Missing roles

The first look at this team shows that we have only two roles represented: Driver and Exec – so as a next step fill out the team's profile by role and characteristic:

Role	Characteristic	Highest Found	Name
Driver	Developer	14	Arthur English
	Director	15	Peter Scotland
	Innovator	15	Arthur English
Planner	Strategist Estimator Scheduler	14	Peter Scotland
Enabler	Resource Manager	12	Arthur English
	Promoter	14	Arthur English
	Negotiator	12	Sarah Welsh
Exec	Producer	13	Sarah Welsh
	Coordinator	13	Sarah Welsh
	Maintainer	13	Sarah Welsh
Controller	Monitor Auditor Evaluator	12	Peter Scotland

We have two Drivers – Arthur English and Peter Scotland – and an Exec, Sarah Welsh. What will be the effects on the way the team works of the missing roles?

The most likely effect of this combination is that this team will never finish a project on time or on budget, for two reasons:

1.   They will not plan in detail – no Estimator or Scheduler. This means that they may well set themselves impossible deadlines, or go largely by feel when putting together a cost estimate.

2.   They will not look where they have been in any depth – no Monitor or Evaluator to observe and record progress. This results in a lack of quantified feedback to correct for the poor initial planning.

This does not mean that this team will not be aware that things are slipping, but they will always find good reasons as to why they are late or over cost – the Enabler in both Arthur and Sarah will tell all involved why it could not have been otherwise. This may well be a hard working team combination but it will, in our experience, make little difference to the outcome.

Transfer is the obvious first option, indeed Arthur and Sarah will probably both be picking up the Enabler role for the team as and when they feel the need. The only change you need to propose is that Arthur makes a conscious effort to step forward in the role. While Sarah scored 32, it was not her secondary role preference – Driver scored higher and so this is more likely to be the role she will move to under pressure.

We are still missing a Controller and a Planner. Peter Scotland scores only 30 as a Controller, but it is his secondary role, why can't he pick it up for the team? A closer look at the scores shows that Peter scores a 12 point difference between his primary and his secondary role. As a Controller, the two characteristics concerned with quality issues – Auditor and Evaluator – dominate, while the record keeping and progress control functions of the Monitor are only a lukewarm preference. All you are likely to get is a Driver's simulation of a Controller (see the out of role performance description in Chapter 3).

There is no opportunity to spread the missing roles. A Strategist, without an Estimator or Scheduler, backed by a polarised Driver's role score will not produce a workable plan. Indeed the danger is that if it were attempted, Sarah would be put under pressure and switch to Driver, thus effectively creating a team of three Drivers!

This team need to recruit or co-opt somebody who will apply the disciplines of planning and progress control. There is no reason why Peter cannot contribute and support the new appointee in these roles, provided that he can accept the need to defer to the other, rather than simply drive for a quick solution.

Looking at our team, we also need to consider the effect of duplicated roles. Will the two Drivers co-operate and share, or will they each battle for their own vision of the future? The flexibility and ability to generate enthusiasm of the Enabler which is Arthur's

secondary role may founder against Peter's polarised role preference. On the other hand, they may both share the same vision and
frustrate Sarah by bulldozing their way ahead and refusing to
accept that there may be obstacles. If this team comes under
pressure, Sarah will move to Driver and battle may be well and
truly joined!

If this was your existing team, now would be the time to ask
yourself:

1. Who gets passed the 'out of role' tasks at present?

2. Do the tasks get done or has the team a real blind spot?

3. Is there an obvious candidate for transfer, or have you to
   make a compromise choice?

4. Role spread – what would you like those concerned to
   attempt for the team?

5. How are you going to get them to work together and
   contribute in this role?

6. If you need to recruit or co-opt, how are you going to get the
   team to propose this approach? What is possible in the
   current climate within your organisation?

7. Have you anyone in mind who could go through the self
   analysis questionnaire?

8. How do those individuals who have the same role preference get on with each other? Will they role share successfully, or will one dominate and suppress the other?

Team stress

You can now make a start on working out the total stress risk factor
for your team, using the scoring basis outlined in the previous
chapter.

1. Write down the role opposites first. In our team above, we
   have:

   Driver – Arthur English v Sarah Welsh – Exec
   Exec – Sarah Welsh v Peter Scotland – Driver

   Opposites score: 4 points.

2. Look at individualism: When asked, Arthur rated himself
   more towards independence. He selected Cautious – he had

definitely had his fingers burnt in the past, more often than not. Score 4.

Peter and Sarah both plumped for Anchor as their rating. Score $2 \times 2 = 4$.

Individualism score: 8 points.

3. Study role shifts under pressure: Only Arthur was deemed to show no change under pressure, although he felt sure he was moving to the Enabler role and becoming more flexible.

   Sarah seemed to change under pressure. Her speech became more cautious and precise and she took longer thinking through what she wanted to say before speaking. She, however, felt that she had to put more effort into selling her ideas under pressure and was therefore more like an Enabler.

   Peter felt that he paid more attention to detail under pressure so was more likely to move to Controller – his secondary role. The others were not sure – he did occasionally erupt as a Driver and they thought this was a sign of pressure.

   Score it the way the team members feel about themselves – we will look at how they communicated in the next section; Arthur moved to Enabler, his secondary role – a natural shift, 3 points.

   Sarah moved to Enabler – an unnatural shift, as her secondary role was Driver, 5 points.

   Peter moved to Controller – a natural shift, 3 points.

   Role shift total: 11 points

4. Assess communication style: Neither Peter nor Arthur had seen Sarah as an Exec, they both thought she was most probably an Enabler – bright and fluent in speech, who always got her point made.

   That Peter was a Driver was equally difficult for Sarah and Arthur to deduce. They thought of him as a Planner – the slow careful precision of speech, also reflected in his meticulous writing style.

   Arthur came across as what he was, a Driver – fast thinking, somewhat pushy, occasionally rubbing people up the wrong way without noticing.

Ask the team members how *they* perceive each others' communication style when deciding this score. If there is a consensus and it matches, score 1; if they all agree it doesn't match the role, score it as a 5; if there is no single view and people are not sure, score 3.

Arthur English – Driver as Driver – 1.

Sarah Welsh – Exec as Enabler – 5.

Peter Scotland – Driver as Planner – 5.

Communication style total: 11 points.

Team stress total: 34

Divide by number in the team – 3.

Team Stress Risk Factor: 11.3

Our example team is a team at risk. They have a high potential for stress. But you must always remember that it is only a *potential* risk. If these three have worked together fairly successfully for a number of years, they may well be used to each other and have developed team coping mechanisms to counter the effects. Adding a team member, who everyone agrees fits and prefers the Planner role, to this team should reduce the stress score and boost the team's performance.

Look at your team – if you do not have enough information to work out the stress risk factor, ask yourself, as you prepare for the first team meeting:

1. Role opposites – is this a homogeneous or a true composite team with four or five role types? Be prepared to explain what could happen to the rest of the team. Have there been any signs of this in the past?

2. Independence v team player: does everyone really want to play? If they are truly independent, should you counsel them before the meeting to find out what's behind their result?

3. Role shifts and communication style – who could be under stress? How can you get them to be open about it? Does the team change under pressure?

Team goals and objectives

While you talk to the others about their results as you prepare for the meeting, gently sound the team out to see if everyone thinks you are a real team. If there is little consensus, or you are not sure in your mind how to define a real team, ask yourself these questions:

1. How closely do you work together away from the team meeting?

Think hard about this one: Do you assign complete projects to an individual or assign tasks for the team to make a full contribution? In many cases we have found one person accepting a 'task' which required them to develop and outline strategy, make decisions as to the best approach to adopt, solve problems, determine feasibility, gain resources, get commitment from those outside the team, negotiate, produce the output, write the reports, and determine the quality standards. The only thing they didn't set was the deadline for achieving all this! All too often, when they returned to the team with their creation, the team immediately wanted to change things. Sometimes this may be merely annoying cosmetic detail, at others the team will insist on a revision which overrides fundamental elements of the work.

If this happens in your team, start thinking now how you are going to change. This is not team working. It is only critique by committee!

2.   Does anyone feel left out or even excluded from the team's activities? (You may have a team within a 'team'.)

This may start as: 'Martin's not interested in this part of it. No need to involve him, it will just be a waste of his time.' All right, as long as it does not become a habit.

Or: 'We don't all need to get together on this one, Jim and I will look into it and decide.' True if it is a single task. Do not let it become an exclusive partnership.

Take care! Deciding what other people should want is the first step on the road to destroying their contribution. This is one way people become indifferent to the needs of your team. Let them decide. If they decide to opt out too often, challenge that as well.

3.   What do you see as the goals and objectives of the team? Do the others agree?

Have you ever formalised it? Many management teams we looked at were more concerned with survival than achieving their original goal. This may be natural in a recession, but it places a restraint on your ability to move forward again as things improve. The companies that win in the bad times, prosper luxuriantly in the good. They never forget they have a goal.

When one Japanese firm had achieved its goal of a 99.99 per cent quality standard – 0.01 per cent failure rate, they immediately set themselves a new goal: 99.999 per cent – 0.001 per cent failure rate. The goal was just as important as the achievement.

4. What progress has the team made to date? (Why not ask the Controller, if you have one?)
    You may all be working terribly hard, the quality of your work is of the highest. Yet, in measurable terms, how far have you moved towards your goal?
    Some project based activities are easy to measure. Other teams set great store by financial or market share targets. Even if your team's activities cannot foresee an end point, there must be some milestones along the way. If you haven't got any, then it is time you got your Planner to set some. (If you have not got a Planner... that is probably why you cannot answer the question!).

SETTING THE AGENDA

Prepare a normal meeting agenda, but do not attempt to publish it! Take the topics to be covered and try to assign them by role. Group them together, changing the order to the following role sequence:

1. Enabler – because they will get the meeting going and talk about achievements!

2. Exec – to raise the issues of the day and ensure a fair share of the workload.

3. Planner – to clarify the future implications.

4. Driver – to problem solve and move to agree decisions.

5. Controller – to cover quality issues and summarise the agreed actions.

Your first meeting agenda should only cover the following:

Introduction

This is *not* a training session! It is a time to share experiences and ideas and to begin to find a more satisfying and productive way of working together.

Start by asking each member to tell the team what they found – ask the Controller to take notes for everyone. If you don't have a

Controller, try to co-opt someone to take notes for the meeting. Do they agree the process was helpful? Did the results seem valid?

What we found

Give everyone a copy of the team profile. If you all agree, also exchange role score sheets. If you cannot agree to do this, you must stop and find out why. Effectively, you have someone who does not want to take part in the team's development. It will help to remind the waverer(s) that this is not about skill, suitability, promotion prospects or any other performance based criteria. It is only about letting the team understand which tasks you prefer doing, supported by an attempt to improve team interaction and to reduce the potential for stress by seeing the other person's point of view.

The objective of the exercise is to let everyone be different and equal, contributing where they will feel most comfortable. It may also help to get things going if you talk through a summary using the notes taken while preparing for this meeting.

Moderator

Even though they may all have read the book, once you have talked over the findings you should introduce the concept of the Moderator leadership style and passing the leadership baton. It may take quite some time before the 'management speak' approach starts to go away!

In nearly all the teams we have worked with, particularly in the phase of preparation for this first meeting, when we have discussed what the sponsor of the team is going to do, they will say things like: 'I'll get Joe to cover that.' Or 'With a bit of a push from me, I'm sure Jenny could help there.'

They are still thinking in terms of getting people to do things, rather than about encouraging contribution. A Moderator oriented thinker might say instead: 'That's a planning task. Let's see if we can get Joe to pick it up for the team.' Or 'Jenny is our newest Exec. She will need encouragement from the others to contribute there.'

Too much management thinking can be one step (or even no step) away from manipulating people. There is no room in a team built of equals for thinking of people as pawns to be pushed around as in a game. Drivers and Planners especially, please note!

The work

Talk about how they should try to set the agenda, comparing the old approach with your role based attempt.

What do they want to do first? (NB: they will probably be unsure – tell them it should all become clearer as the meeting goes on.) Try to get an agreement to include time in the Enabler's section of the agenda at which you can try to:

1. Get a commitment from everyone to look at their role and characteristic advice again.

2. Find a task suited to each team member's primary role which they know the team would not ordinarily do. It will help if you have decided upon your own proposed actions before the meeting. Explain why you have picked these particular actions to encourage the others to open up their minds.

Redraw the agenda based on everyone's input. In other words, get the team to set their own meeting agenda by role – then pass the baton to the role they select to pick it up first!

Sit back, but whenever the meeting grinds to a halt, or someone tries to impose a judgment from the chair, move in and moderate to get contribution and stimulate the realisation as to what they are doing to each other!

Remember: it's the team's meeting – they will have to do this again many times to be successful. They must run their own meeting to take ownership of the team of equals concept. Gentle prompting rather than management direction is what is needed here – this first meeting is a coaching not a training situation.

DEVELOP AS A TEAM

Training for the team to work as a team is not what is needed at this time. Team development will only take time, patience, persistence and practice. Each team member will need to make allowances (especially for their role opposites!) and to try to support the others as they learn and adjust. Concentrate only on maintaining openness and in trying to find positive reactions to problems and pressure – this could be a task your Exec may wish to take on for the team.

To develop as a team, place the emphasis on developing each individual in their role. The more comfortable they feel in their role, the more they will contribute to the team. The key to role comfort lies in developing the task oriented skills and techniques needed by each role. To identify these, we start by looking at the characteristics which make up the role.

Our view is that being different and equal is the only way to move forward effectively. This emphasis may seem to be diametrically opposed to conventional leadership and management training wisdom, which concentrates on plugging gaps in knowledge and trying to eliminate weaknesses.

We believe the team of equals approach is more realistic in its aims. The intention is to confirm and reinforce team members in their role position, building on the strengths of their preferences, rather than equip them to take on any task the team may require of them. After all, when you have learned to work together as a team, why should you feel the need to be able to attempt all the tasks which a team has been assembled to tackle? That is why the job has been assigned to a team instead of a multi-talented individual in the first place.

How then, you may well ask, are they going to acquire the broad spread of abilities and skills to be a successful manager or leader? Surely we are limiting them to a restrictive specialisation? Training must be good for you; after all, that is why we send people on courses. Many people seem to believe that, to use Phineas Barnum's famous dictum on publicity and apply it to training: 'All training is good training'. As their justification goes – you never know when you might need it.

Cast your mind back to any management training (rather than functional skills) you may have received. It may well have been inspiring. You may even have felt privileged to have been selected to attend. But *be honest*, how many of the techniques you were taught, which were designed to 'round you out' as a manager, have you ever used? Look again: our researches have showed that only those techniques which match tasks related to primary or secondary role preferences get used in the long term.

In a successful team, the key management skill to acquire is that of the Moderator. The better you get at moderating, the greater the contribution you will generate. Learning how to let the Planner produce the best plan the team can produce from the people within it and those with whom it interacts may well be the hardest thing you will ever do. It would (in many cases) help to have someone at your side operating in the same way as the slave who accompanied the Roman General on his triumph through the streets of Rome. Crouched beside the great General the slave would whisper again and again: 'You are only mortal'. Many a manager who feels that he or she has to provide the definitive input to every task or decision, could use someone beside them to remind them that, even if they can accept that they are not a god, they aren't Superman either!

One Driver of our acquaintance, a powerful, enthusiastic entrepreneur finally accepted the value of this message and co-opted his secretary to work as his team's Exec. In addition, he made the particular point of giving her an absolute dispensation to tell him to shut up and listen, because there was work to be done! He needed this help to stop trampling all over the contributions from the rest of the team, which had virtually dried up as a result of too much direction on every issue.

ROLE COMFORT

Apart from being a practised and skilful Moderator, all team members should seek to enhance their contribution to the team through training which reinforces their role and helps to improve their level of comfort in the role. Preference shows you your aspirations, but until you achieve a comfortable state within the role, you may well express a preference mainly on your perception of your personal circumstances or your environment which leaves you saying, 'I feel I must...'.

The key to achieving role comfort is task oriented training. For example, if after 20 years as an accountant you are finally appointed managing director and see the need to change the things you do to fit your perception of how a managing director behaves, you may express a preference for the Driver role, but it will take time to achieve any significant level of comfort: you will need to grow into the job (and suffer the growing pains!), a familiar process to many. Look at those tasks within the role which make you feel uncomfortable and select a course of training to help. One new managing director may find presentation skills useful another feel the need for some formal training in goal setting.

As all the characteristics within the roles are based on tasks a successful team has to do, identifying training directions is quite simple. You do not need to wait for the Controller to identify the training need as he or she audits the team's performance; just ask your Enabler to identify, propose (and even source) the training which you think would help you from the role based advice which follows:

Driver: developer, director, innovator

The Driver's natural orientation is forward looking. The solving of problems and the handling of change are subjects to which they will respond. Adding a sound structural approach to this preference will increase the Driver's contribution to the team, not least because it may stop them leaping to an intuitive conclusion quite so rapidly and prepare them to seek out and accept input from the Planner and Controller. The Developer characteristic will benefit from the study of goal setting and management; the Director from the study of decision making techniques and change management; the Innovator from problem solving and brainstorming techniques and the process of their facilitation.

Planner: strategist, estimator, scheduler

Strategic planning is an obvious choice for the Strategist characteristic. For the Estimator, forward looking research disciplines, such as desk and market research techniques, should be supported by training in forecasting, modelling approaches, risk analysis, and target setting techniques. The Scheduler may benefit from project planning techniques such as critical path analysis and formalised scheduling approaches. Much of this may link to training in computer based techniques, from the use of simple spreadsheet software, to full blown project design and management suites.

Enabler: resource manager, promoter, negotiator

Communication skills are vital to the Enabler, not just on a one-to-one basis, but also in the wider context of public relations. Public relations on behalf of the team also applies to communicating with those within the company affected by the team's activities: as teams sometimes seem to forget that these activities may have an impact on several hundred people around them, who will benefit from being aware of what is going on. The Resource Manager may benefit from training in research and prospecting techniques, training techniques and approaches setting and defining purchase specifications, job specification and recruitment techniques and interview training. The Promoter, apart from the obvious subjects such as presentation techniques, promotion, public relations and selling skills training, may also make good use of training in motivational techniques and the understanding of body language

– non verbal communication. Putting structure into the Negotiator's approach through a negotiating course can also help them answer many of the charges of 'giving things away for nothing' from less flexible members of the team!

Exec: *producer, co-ordinator, maintainer*

People and job skills are the primary training areas for the Exec. Telephone skills training may do more to enhance an Exec's output than time planning for example, although, both may be of benefit. Technical skills training may seem obvious if they are running a printing press, but may be less obvious when in an office environment. Proper training to get the most out of computer aids – advanced word processing or spreadsheet design for example – may raise the quality and speed of their co-ordination and production tasks. Support this with training in performance management, job design and procedure writing and the Exec will demonstrate the true value of the role. Do not neglect the Maintainer skills of counselling and coaching which will benefit from a structured approach – much time can be saved if techniques of ventilation, problem identification and stress reduction are understood and applied to the benefit of everyone.

Controller: *monitor, auditor, evaluator*

The Auditor and Evaluator characteristics will both benefit from training in management audits and quality control techniques. The Monitor from report writing, information systems and progress control techniques. What may be less obvious is to train the Controller in problem and change management: this is the key to the successful implementation of planned change, providing the feedback from which all the other roles will benefit.

One last thought on training – the Exec in the Sales office may look at the apparent glamour of the salesman's life and express the preference to move to be an Enabler; the Enabler may be wilting under the pressure of the salesman's job and wish to become a Planner in Marketing; the Planner may have reached a point when they would prefer just to set strategy and take decisions as a Driver without getting stuck working out all the boring detail; the Driver may get frustrated at facing the same problems day after day and begin to move towards Controller where they can monitor other people's efforts to instigate change; the Controller could reach the point at which getting one's head down handling the routine and the co-ordination of other peoples efforts as an Exec seems awfully attractive.

The grass is always greener and this may be reflected in some of the secondary role preferences in your team. Unless they have been asked to step forward consciously in this role for the team, it is better to concentrate on becoming the best contributor in their primary role for the team and decide the training plans accordingly.

We have found that training within your preferred role can revitalise your interest by providing new angles on what you prefer to do *and* it will increase your value to the team, which in a team built of equals will be recognised and acknowledged.

WORKING WITH EACH OTHER

This may seem an obvious thing to do, but many teams we looked at only worked together when they came to their meetings. Their idea of team working was doing the task or tasks assigned to them by the team and then reporting back on progress (or lack of it) at the next meeting.

Managers and team leaders were often under the impression that working together on a task was more akin with hand holding than sharing. Terms such as duplication of effort and inefficient use of resources, or comments such as 'They work faster alone' and 'It only needs one person to do that' (whatever it happened to be) displayed a genuine concern for productivity.

Yet looking at how the team worked in practice, we saw that all the statements could be shown to be at best half truths and certainly did not apply universally, especially when the total time taken to complete the tasks was calculated:

- Duplication of Effort: Working together on tasks which include elements of communication, planning or reporting often benefit from two team members working together. Communication can be tested and understanding improved; more data can be gathered and analysed before being collated; the generation of ideas improved by input from the associations triggered in two minds working in parallel. Fewer revisions are needed as the output is more balanced.

- Inefficient Use of Resources: Two people working at one keyboard may seem inefficient, but each is able to monitor and enhance the other's input and contribute to the solution of problems; the rate of clean, usable input may even increase. Sharing a car may reduce flexibility, but gives extended opportunities to talk things over in what would otherwise be dead time.

- They work faster alone: How much thought does this task require and would two heads be better than one? While there are tasks which benefit from a lack of interruption, there are just as many in a teamworking situation where two or more people working together get it done faster, not least because they do it right *once*. Even if it is a boring, repetitive assembly task, as mundane as stuffing envelopes for example, dividing the work amongst the team and keeping the conversation going while you work together, not only makes light of a chore, but often saves valuable meeting time later on.

- It only needs one person to do that: Sending two people to make a sales visit or handle a negotiation is often held up as a typical 'hand holding' activity. Yet two people handling a negotiation may well bring back a better deal, as they provide thinking time for each other when under pressure. As for the sales visit, adding up the cost of two or sometimes three additional sales visits to handle all the queries a customer needs answered before placing an order, instead of sending a salesman and a technician who between them can provide all the necessary information, speaks for itself.

The answer is to use your Planner to the full. Not just to determine if the tasks are to be done sequentially or concurrently, but also to determine which roles need to be actively involved with each of the tasks; which tasks would benefit from role sharing, and when to call the whole team together to provide maximum effort and foster team spirit.

Do not forget that some of the team may be more independent minded than others, but do not let their low need for team contact and support divert you from getting the team to work together, or the team may gradually fall apart.

Case 10: The Individualist

Andrew was a member of a National training team, but he refused to work away from home. He claimed that this was because his mother, with whom he lived, was ill. Initially the team sympathised, but became disillusioned when Andrew took three week holidays in Bermuda and weekend trips in the UK.

The reaction of the team was to become hyper-critical, so that nothing Andrew did was correct or of value, but Andrew remained calm and aloof. He did join the group's quality circle but attended only one meeting – he was not invited to any others.

While Andrew was certainly not a natural team player, in performance terms, there was no reason why he should be, provided that he could convince the group that his way of working still supported the team as a whole. To do this he needed to prove the validity of his contribution, but he showed little concern for what the team thought of him or his work.

He took on more of the mundane teaching tasks for the team, but while these tasks were not popular with the other team members, Andrew's efforts were not generally appreciated. The isolation continued until it could be claimed that there were now two teams, Andrew and the others.

Andrew worked like an Exec and communicated like one, when he communicated at all. His continued inclusion in the team was based on his claim that he could do the job if left alone, but the team had little faith in his technical capability despite his length of experience. He failed in his efforts to develop a new course and in the end just taught, neither superbly nor badly.

The team suffered considerable tension through Andrew's behaviour. Performance suffered as the team began to discuss and complain more and more. Andrew was not unduly concerned or stressed. Letting one member opt out created a sick team, and ensured the failure of the individual, even though he did not suffer personally as he was indifferent to their opinions.

Much of the role development advice given in Chapter 3 is designed to promote the habit of working together. Learning to accept the value of other people's contributions should not be confined to a metaphorical round of applause for a job well done at the team's meetings. The Driver needs to learn to both ask for and to accept the data on which to base a decision from the Controller, the Planner to seek out and make use of information on which to revise and refine a plan from the Enabler or Exec.

Don't be like the computer industry new product team who spent their first meeting setting the meeting dates for the rest of the year – that way lies committeedom! Encourage more contact on a day-to-day basis and you will find that the full team meetings will become shorter yet more productive. You may even reach the stage of effective team working when you will only feel the need to meet when you have something concrete to discuss, plan or decide, instead of just meeting to report progress. The need to communicate via memos should reduce, as the team comes to rely on faster face-to-face (or phone-to-phone) methods. A real team should always be small enough to keep the communication flowing. Working with each other, linked with an understanding of role contribution, rapidly builds effective communications.

8
Making it Work: Management Issues

Management issues may have moved more and more to the forefront of your mind, as you have read on chapter by chapter. Although working as a team may seem entirely logical and supportable in specialised circumstances, a project team for example, by now you may be saying to yourself that this is Utopian fantasy, that real organisations don't work like that and sadly, from the viewpoint of your own experience, you may be right. However, that is only an indication of the handicaps under which many organisations labour. While we have never found a team which did not benefit from the team of equals approach to teamwork, we have found organisations where the management issues caused us to slow, and in one case even forego, implementation of the full programme.

The open and supportive team environment created by a team built of equals requires an organisation to address the following issues in order to avoid a culture clash between a close knit and democratic team (which has become used to speaking its mind on any team issue and expects to talk through and contribute ideas before deciding what is to be done) and the wider management environment (which may still be primarily autocratic in nature and command and control oriented).

- leadership;
- team training;
- the BigTeam Impact;
- single status;
- management authority and responsibility;

■ matrix working.

In facing these issues, you may well discover that the expectations of many of the people within your organisation are already strongly in line with our approach. People are seeking more and more to control their own destinies and to question the wisdom and validity of sweeping dictates issued from somewhere remote up above. Many will have seen television programmes or read about companies which have adopted a more egalitarian team based mode of operation. Hardly a week goes by without some new story being featured: building cars in Scandinavia, washing machines in Philadelphia and electronics in Swansea. The stories are always the same: gains in productivity and job satisfaction in an environment where everyone works together, is encouraged to contribute and is actively listened to by the management. This is an approach in tune with, and a part of, the aspirations of the workforce of the nineties.

Whatever the issue, there are those who will resist change no matter how non-threatening the process, while others seem to go overboard in favour. The response on the one hand may be to raise barriers and retreat behind them. On the other, to grasp the opportunity and make full use of the new approach in all their activities, both in their own teams and in their dealings with others who have not yet been exposed to the concepts. Both extremes can prove disruptive if you are not expecting it: managers who suddenly become democratic and sincerely attempt to work as equals can be just as unsettling to those used to rigid formality as those who compensate by emphasising every difference in status.

In some ways, the creation of the first team built of equals in an organisation is like Pandora's box: once you have opened it you may find it difficult to stop the effects from spreading – not least because everyone wants to do the questionnaire to find out their role! So make sure you understand fully the management issues that may arise as a result.

LEADERSHIP

Those leadership styles which reinforce the position of the leader as someone in charge of, yet not quite a part of the team, be they action- centred or by example oriented, will come under pressure. Assigning the tasks will be considered topics for scrutiny and discussion by the team.

It will become glaringly obvious if the leader attempts to carry the team by picking up an unfair (and probably unachievable) share of the work. Those who depend on a title for their authority, but contribute little may feel similarly pressured. They will be expected to contribute in role, not just delegate and then receive reports.

The main barrier to the Moderator style of leadership is most often insecurity. This exhibits itself in several ways:

- Isolation from the team – a position which rapidly communicates itself to other team members – justified as keeping things on a 'not so thick that you cannot stir' basis.

- Stifling formality and a concentration on procedure. No first names and everything going 'through the chair' are part of this syndrome.

- Demands for loyalty and respect not so much for the person, as for the rank or position that they have been given.

- Insistence on team members working separately. Occasionally this is a deliberate attempt to divide and rule.

- 'Need to know' communication – creating an inner circle and treating some team members as second class citizens.

Any attempt to maintain a barrier between the leader and the team will destroy the team. They will be expecting to be treated as equal status colleagues when working as part of the team, so that a full and open two-way communication becomes possible, releasing the contribution from all members of the team. Silence is one of the first signs of a team member either under stress or opting out.

The change that is required, apart from learning to adopt the moderator style within the team, is primarily to relax! Be less formal, or at least as informal as the organisation's culture will permit. Generate loyalty by displaying a measure of trust. If you do not feel that this trust is reciprocated, then feel free to tackle the issue with all the team present. Try to get them to voice their concerns and, in turn, to express your feelings on the matter. Do not be afraid to raise the issues which are causing you to worry or even just to feel that things could be working better, and try to encourage the rest of the team to do the same. There can be no taboo subjects which adversely affect the working of a team built of equals. Try and accept criticism positively, which in turn will give you the right to criticise based on the understanding that openness is the key to stress reduction and to breaking down the barriers to good communication.

If the leadership style continues to be autocratic and directive, ignoring the contribution to be gained through the Moderator style, the team will become unbalanced and demonstrate a bias which reflects the leader's role preferences.

LEADER'S ROLE EFFECTS

As we have seen in Chapter 5, in a specialist team such as marketing, sales or quality control, the leader should have the characteristics most needed to carry out the primary task. While the very nature of the tasks concerned will reinforce and develop the role characteristics, marketing is best led by a Planner; sales by an Enabler; quality control by a Controller. Put the wrong role in charge and it can be horrific: a Controller in charge of a sales team may kill it with a burden of analysis and reporting. A Driver in charge of a sustained activity may try to change direction too often. A Planner in charge of a production facility may spend too much time working out the future and not enough on present problems.

The traditional approach has been to get the leader to make up perceived deficiencies in the team by training him or her to plug the gaps in their own, or their team's performance profile. These may be obvious to an outsider looking at a single function team and there is no reason why, intellectually, the team leader may not agree and accept the need for this training. They may even ask for specialised leadership training in the belief that this acknowledges that they have been chosen to lead and that this will make them more promotable as a result. It ignores the fact that changes in behavioural characteristics *take time*. They do occur – we have all seen someone grow into a job – but the more mature the person the less likely they are to change quickly enough.

The result is that teams demonstrate the effects of the leader's role preferences, simply because the leader believes that those tasks should have emphasis. After all they may well be essential to the leader's way of working and have been the foundation of their success, which put them in the leadership position in the first place. If the leader is running a specialist team, they may well spend all their time hiring in their own image; making sure that they get what they believe is the right sort of person for the job. This in itself may not be damaging, but it does explain why so much emphasis in management training is on generalised task-based processes, which on closer analysis turn out to be based on the need to plug the performance drain occasioned by these role based gaps.

Look at the sort of courses that are used to train managers, then think of the 15 characteristics needed by a successful team:

decision making	presentation skills
target setting	negotiating
problem solving	time planning
forecasting	counselling
estimating	quality audits
scheduling	report writing
buying	assessment/evaluation.

Any manager could expect to go on one of these courses, or find them as part of their management training. They may be exposed to the techniques, but if the role doesn't match, few of the techniques will ever be used. The end result is that, if the team is being run to reflect the preferences of the leader, the consequences will be there for all to see.

The driver's team

At first sight, a Driver makes an ideal manager of change. After all they actively seek it and insist upon it. Decisions are made fast. Problems are welcomed, 'It's not a problem, it's an opportunity' is a typical Driver saying. This is the ideal team to bulldoze something through.

You can always spot the Driver's team, it's the one that keeps being reorganised in some way. There will always be some new approach to be adopted which will fix the problems created by the old way of doing things.

Drivers are good organisers and have no inhibitions about making demands on their teams. This team can be a very stimulating place to be, providing you can stand up to the rough handling that may take place, especially if there is more than one Driver on the team. Everything has to happen at speed. It all works to a deadline or a target date. Feasibility is assumed, because achieving the goal is part of the Driver's required future.

Driver led teams thrive in crisis management situations. (If there isn't a crisis they often seem to provoke one!) They will break down the barriers to progress and don't let precedent or procedure stand in their way. If you want to break new ground or operate in unexplored territory, a Driver led team would seem to be the answer. But they do tend to need another team sweeping up behind them.

Drivers are best suited to leading new project teams or running development oriented sections. If they are required to take on another management role, try and find a Driver with a strong secondary role – not more than six points different to the Driver role score – and assign according to the recommendations for the secondary role in the next chapter.

The Planner's team

Teams led by Planners produce meticulous work, but they can take a long time to get going. There is always more research to be done, more information to gather, the latest estimates to assess. Everyone will be consulted to input to the planning process. Much emphasis is placed on good information systems and detailed planning exercises.

This team should certainly know where its going, once it makes up its mind where that's likely to be. Once set on the track, the leader will insist they work to the plan, until it's time for the next planning exercise, when resources will tend to be diverted to prepare the next plan.

If you see a team in a medium to large company situation that has two productive periods in the year and the rest of the time doesn't achieve very much, it's probably led by a Planner. First the team will be diverted to produce the budget, then six months later, they will be diverted to revise the strategic plan.

Marketing teams should always be led by a Planner – no other role will handle the necessary forward looking research, or produce the fully detailed support packages required, particularly for technical product lines. Other future based teams – research teams, medical teams, legal teams, all of whom have to anticipate future positions and plan courses of action to counter threats, also benefit from a Planner at the head.

The Enabler's team

Teams led by Enablers are lively places to be. Everyone has a great time! The people on this team go on more courses than anyone else; they hold meetings in fantastic locations and always have a budget to do things others find impossible.

This team is always just about to be very successful. This new opportunity or that new product will transform the team's performance. Of course, next time it may well be a different opportunity and a modification of the original product idea which is essential for success.

If the role is shared with Driver as the secondary role this team may well be very successful in reality, but you will have to run very fast to keep up!

The classic jobs for the Enabler are in the interface between a company and its customers and suppliers. Buying and selling will both benefit from the Enabler's leadership. The other key tasks for the Enabler are the promotion of change – they are the best team leaders to handle the human interface of a company move, for example – and the handling of Public Relations.

The Exec's team

A team led by an Exec is a busy place to be. There is always plenty of work to be done and the team leader will see that everyone does their fair share.

Non-conformists beware: this leader will not be sympathetic. By all means propose improvements in procedures, but don't actually promulgate change. Personal problems are the only ones to get serious consideration in this team: the amount of time the leader makes available to counsel and support those, who others might dismiss as weak links or inadequate performers, seems limitless.

Execs are best at leading teams which require sustained effort in support of others and the organisation. The sales office, the production unit, the personnel department are all ideal Exec led environments.

The Controller's team

A team led by a Controller will always have immaculate paperwork. This team works by the rules and seems to spend most of it time trying to institute even more rules and regulations. They may appear capable of spending more effort on one detail of an issue than they spend on the rest of the project.

The future is only of interest to this team if it can be made to conform to the patterns of the past. Previous mistakes will be analysed in great detail and controls instituted to prevent the same mistake happening twice. The result, if not curtailed by the protests of those outside the team, will be a team that proceeds very methodically to a pedestrian conclusion.

Controllers are natural leaders for those specialised teams which rely on following procedures to the letter: accounts, quality control, banking, finance, conveyancing. If there is an administration emphasis, without the need for decision or the exercise of discretion, the Controller will run the team along the preordained track.

If leadership is allowed to dominate and the leader's role preferences are imposed on the team's plans and activities, then teams will perform in the predictable manner outlined above. Provided that the working environment does not require a response to change, four of these teams will work at their specialist tasks fairly effectively and the fifth will spend most of its time trying to provoke change. It is only when, as always happens in the real world, teams are faced with the challenge of the new or a need to develop a response to changed circumstances, that each of these teams will need to behave like a real team.

It is then that they will need the contribution to be made by each of the five roles and they must plan and respond as a complete team. The leader must then reduce his or her influence on the team to bring it back into balance.

To practice the Moderator style does not have to wait until a new challenge creates the need for a team, for which it is an essential element for success. It is just as valid for everyday use in a specialist team to stimulate contribution from every level and to produce a full team effort.

TEAM TRAINING

If training the leaders, rounding out with theory to make up for lack of experience and plugging the knowledge gaps, is not the whole answer, then once you have put together a complete team and got them started, training the whole team to work as a team must be the logical progression.

It should work, but very often the method is inappropriate, not least when the team is taken out of its working context and put into an artificial environment which is both physically and mentally stressful. Much of this training is based upon team tasks designed to ensure that the team has to work together physically to achieve the completion of the task. This is intended to bring the team together yet, all too often, the opposite occurs. As one stressed out executive put it to us on his return from an S.A.S style 'teambuilding weekend' experience: 'This method may well be applicable when the team is from a stressed or hyper-active organisation and the culture is best described as only the survivors will succeed!'

For many teams this method is simply irrelevant. Indeed, if it ends up becoming competitive, it can even result in the 'winners' – usually those who were physically stronger and fitter – becoming elitist and those who had a tough time being seen as losers or weak links. Having to drag an exhausted colleague up a mountain, or even worse, see them carried off to recover while the team goes on, is unlikely to make any real contribution to team cohesion.

Weekends away in a challenging environment, or worse still encouraging open aggression and competition playing executive war games, should be limited to providing an opportunity for *individuals* to learn more about themselves and their potential contribution to a team through the process of self discovery. If you wish to try and help one team member feel more capable of making a contribution, working with a team of strangers instead of their own team colleagues, whose experience and status they may still find inhibiting, may prove a confidence booster. In this case the people involved with the experiences of winning and losing, surviving and failing are left behind at the end of the course. The (hopefully) more self aware individual can return to their teams with their reputation intact, irrespective of how well they fared under the stressful conditions imposed by the course. One simple plea: pick carefully who you choose to send and get your Enabler and Controller to research and vet the courses.

The main barrier to achieving a successful team through Outward Bound style training, is that so many so-called team training approaches are last years leadership course in a new marketing package. Our advice is to read the small print: do they talk about leadership experiences, command tasks, management confidence, teams including their manager, or open leadership? If so, while no doubt very sincere in their beliefs, they are still playing leaders and followers.

The change in emphasis required is not so dynamic and is perhaps not so much fun, but can be very fulfilling in the long term. The development needs of a team built of equals are those of any team which has to operate as an effective unit. The soccer team and rugby team, (while not real teams in our sense), provide the pointer: they have a coach to keep the team fit and to help develop the team working skills and techniques. A team coach for the team, a trainer for individual skills, knowledge and technique is thus the change in orientation which will initiate an effective team development programme.

Coaching skills often appear diametrically opposed to traditional management. The first reaction of many line managers to a coaching course is that it is too soft, takes too long and doesn't seem to go anywhere in particular. This is because coaching recognises that the strongest influence on a person's development is their experience of doing the job and that coaching must, therefore, take place within the work environment dealing with real problems and issues. Thus to achieve development as a team, one cannot get very far by doing things to them outside the team's work situation. Instead, time should be taken to review and counsel at regular intervals. The Controller observing the group as Auditor is the best source for information to start the review, the Exec the best person to moderate the review session.

Resist pressure to divert this time for other purposes. It may be so much simpler to train rather than take the time to moderate and ask the team those questions which will start everyone thinking in a positive direction. Yet if team development is your aim, generating the realisations as to how the team can help itself to develop can be the most rewarding route to team achievement.

THE BIGTEAM IMPACT

The impact of the thinking and the management style which underlies the team of equals approach can affect the command hierarchy of BigTeam environment in one of two ways:

- If it is seen as a threat to status and a dilution of power, the barriers will rise, and there will be a culture clash. Those at the top may well consider the idea of working as equals and transferring the leadership baton by role to fit the task being attempted to be the first steps on the road to anarchy. Teams may end up operating independently towards their own goals even to the point of being in conflict with the rest of the organisation.

- If it is seen as a major opportunity to secure better communication and productivity, it will provide the Big Team leader with an approach which allows them to make a positive contribution and achieve involvement at any desired level.

As to what can happen when the barriers go up, the following case study will illustrate:

Case 11: The Privatised Service

A local authority had privatised a major service function, employing over a hundred people. They had begun to use the language of the commercial world, but this was only a veneer, covering a rigid and autocratic bureaucracy. The Chief Executive was a BigTeam leader in the paternalistic mould: 'Think of us all as just one big team here.'

The marketing end of the organisation worked for the Administration Director and consisted of a small team which produced a catalogue of the services and supplies. This had been a very low status task, as everyone knew that the real work of gaining business was done by the Chief Executive through his network of contacts in local government. As part of the endeavour to create a more active and aware organisation, the marketing team was chosen to be the pilot for a team development initiative.

After some misgivings at the start, the team responded well. They were led by a bright woman in her late twenties with lots of energy, who was an Enabler/Exec role combination. Within the team they had all the roles except that of Driver, which they filled by recruiting a member from one of the purchasing groups, who also contributed the functional skills of print buying to the team.

The team were held at arms length by the senior management – the justification for this barrier being: 'Leave them alone and we will see what they can do.' As things progressed, there was an underlying buzz within the lower strata of the organisation that this team was working well and doing great things (the enthusiasm of the team's two Enablers saw to that). Unfortunately, it became apparent that the team's Driver had most probably been pushed on them, with a sigh of relief, by his colleagues. He was looked on as a junior and thus was ignored by those outside the team when he attempted to raise the team's influence and stature, in line with his perception of the value of the work being achieved. Yet he was innovative, quite happy to see things change and often pushed the team to a decision without reference to the more and more remote seeming authority. With coaching, the team grew in confidence and effectiveness within their own function area, as they got in tune with their roles and with each other. The team assured everyone that they would be finished on time and within budget. They conformed to the rather formal reporting style and so were left alone until the great day when they were to present their project to the management team consisting of five function heads and the Chief Executive.

The meeting started warmly. The material was a great improvement on anything the organisation had ever attempted to do in the past. Until it began to dawn on the Chief Executive that this team had, by achieving its brief, created a major new marketing method for the service, capable of wider exploitation and circulation than the old boy network which he used to control over 90 per cent of the business. Here was a team, all of them under thirty telling him how to run his operation. He began to look for holes in what they had achieved, and once he started in this direction the rest of the management team joined in.

At this point the team's Controller began to moderate the meeting, recording the points made and passing them to the Driver on his left, who often scribbled on them before passing them on to the team leader. After a a period of helpful moderation by the team, the management team ran out of steam. The Enabler summarised and then began to answer and justify the team's position on every point. Their mutual confidence was too much for the Chief Executive, who thanked them for all their efforts and drew the meeting to a close.

It was later decided that, while the experiment in team development was a qualified success, it would be impractical on a wider scale, until certain unspecified 'other changes' had taken place.

With hindsight the signs were all there to be seen from the beginning. The organisation was excessively bureaucratic, status ridden and formal. The Chief Executive was called 'Mr ***', even by members of the management team who had worked for him for years. They in turn expected this level of formality and respect for their time earned authority from their subordinates. The experience of being handled, even gently, by such a junior team who worked so well together and supported each other when attacked instead of kowtowing to the mandarin, was, from their cultural viewpoint, disruptive of discipline.

As for the team, their teamwork coach counselled them through the period of disappointment, but three of them decided over the next year they were ready for a career move to a more open and less formal environment as a result. The others have been gradually reabsorbed into the old culture.

The impact on a BigTeam that attempts to isolate a team, working as a team built of equals within itself, can be similar to putting a bandage over an infection and hoping it will go away. It will either be stifled, or it will break out, where you least expect it, in a rash of questioning, discussion and unexpected initiative. This in the right environment is perfectly healthy, but in a BigTeam which is dependent on hierarchy and formality and motivated by the symbols of status and the exercise of power, this may well be regarded as a formula for revolution.

If the leader of a BigTeam is truly concerned to make his people just one big team, then the team of equals approach provides an opportunity to fix many of the problems faced by such a leader. In part, they are the mirror image of the problems generated deliberately by the isolationist divide and rule policies of those who feel threatened:

- The leader has difficulty sounding out grass roots opinion – people tell the leader what they think they want to hear.

- If the leader attends a meeting, all concerned defer to his input, or make only a token attempt to discuss the leader's proposals. Contribution from junior team members at such meetings virtually dries up.

- Communication in its true sense – a two way traffic – is poor. Rumour and the grapevine are rampant. Paper based communication systems proliferate in an attempt to compensate.

- Problems become crises before the leader gets to know about them. This can leave the leader perpetually playing the role of troubleshooter in the eyes of subordinates and thus the appearance of the leader, anywhere but in his or her office, is considered a cause for apprehension.

- Motivation methods become global in approach and are hit and miss as a result.

Even if there are no plans to compress the organisation's hierarchical structure, the creation of series of teams which have an understanding of the way teams work will provide an effective communication network for the BigTeam:

- Setting decision guidelines and policy limits for the teams' Drivers will improve response and control.

- Providing input to the teams' Planners and reviewing those plans will improve forecasting and knowledge of intentions.

- Briefing the teams' Enablers will ensure that the whole team get the best and most enthusiastic transmission of the brief.

- Quietly talking over staff motivation issues with the Execs will give the best feedback of staff morale.

- Relying on the teams' Controllers for reports and training them to achieve common reporting standards will produce more reliable and consistent information.

These effects can be achieved without stepping out of the leader's office.

To achieve the full benefit the leader must become part of their own team, fully understanding their role and acquiring the skills of a Moderator. The Moderator style was specifically developed in the seventies to allow managers from the highest to the lowest levels of an organisation to participate in meetings while generating a full contribution from even the most junior subordinate. This does not bar the leader from making their contribution in role, indeed they will be expected to come forward as appropriate. Sitting as a silent observer can be just as stultifying to a team unsure of themselves, so try not to end up as the spectre at the feast. From where the team stand, they are in the same position as when seeking to accommodate a new member who they are not too sure will play by the same rules, however many protestations they make to the contrary!

SINGLE STATUS

While the BigTeam may contain levels of hierarchy from the top to the bottom of an organisation, there is no reason why working as a team built of equals cannot be extremely beneficial when integrated into the management philosophy adopted for the BigTeam.

However the effect on those involved of working in a series of teams as an equal contributor, each interacting at different levels of the organisation which contains members of different status, may well create pressure for elimination of differentials and the adoption of a single status philosophy wherever practicable.

The concept of value is becoming more important than the trappings of status. After all is said and done, why should a highly skilled shift operator, running a multi million pound process in a small team and whose skill and dedication have a major impact on the company's quality and profit, lose a day's pay if he falls sick after twenty years' service, while his 16 year old daughter gets a sick pay entitlement after one month's work in the office? Who contributes more value to the organisation?

The success and productivity of Japanese companies has placed pressure on management worldwide to review the benefits of a move towards a more democratic approach valuing contribution. It has placed similar pressure on unions to seek an end to demarcation battles which were costing their members jobs. What started with paying lip service to the concept, by closing the separate manager's canteen for example, has developed to the point where companies such as Rover cars, (the inheritors of the old British Leyland plants, who were notorious for the time lost through industrial disputes in the 1960s and were, felt by many, impossible to change as the positions of both sides were so entrenched), have announced the intention of becoming single status organisations.

Only those who see single status working as an erosion of privileges will see any threat in treating those they work with in a team as equals, if only for the duration of the team exercise. If you observe the team from a higher rung of the status ladder, look on it as an opportunity to raise the rest of the team to your level, rather than as a case of the team dragging you down to what you perceive as their's and you will not go far wrong. Those at the bottom looking up, who were traditionally suppressed, benefit from the experience. It is heartening to see a young team member who has been asked to moderate for the team for the first time, taking the team through a task which relates to a role they prefer. They may make a mess of it, but no one can take away from them the fact that they were given their chance to make things work better.

The approach adopted in creating a successful team can thus be seen as totally supportive of moves towards a single status organisation.

MANAGEMENT AUTHORITY AND RESPONSIBILITY

Almost inevitably, those who have been management trained and worked hard to achieve their present positions feel a twinge of anxiety at the thought of making even a temporary transfer of leadership.

Just listen to the phrases: 'Stepping down' 'Abdicating responsibility,' 'Letting go of the reins.' The first two smack of relinquishing a throne, the last implies that team will behave like a horse and bolt off into the blue if not restrained and directed! Yet a good team meeting passes the baton of leadership at each role change in the agenda like a well run relay race. A team member who has perhaps been waiting impatiently for their turn as moderator can boost the team's activity rate again and generate a fresh burst of ideas and output. The logic is inescapable. Compare the performance of a relay team with that of a mile runner: only the best can achieve a sub-four minute time even now, while a 4×400 metre relay team gets close to three minutes by passing the baton to fresh runner who takes a running start.

The only risk is that by not letting go the leader will act as a brake on their team: a leader who grabs all the tasks because of a lack of trust in the team's capabilities usually dooms it to failure. A leader who delegates all the tasks and only analyses reports of progress may have a similar effect. In our examination of the reports on the causes of team failure in many teams, the assignment of responsibility for failure had little effect on the outcome in terms of either penalties or the future career moves affecting the team's leader. Some leaders managed to offload blame onto the team, others carried the can. In some cases those who tried to shed the blame were penalised, in others those who stood up for their team were apparently rewarded despite failure. The effects were not predictable. So our advice is simple: ignore any thoughts of failure and get on with running a team built of equals. It will be far better to spend your efforts coaching all concerned to moderate well for the team when it comes to their turn.

Does this detract from the leader's authority? What about discipline? Does this mean we have to hold the whole team responsible? Joint responsibility at the top is more easily accepted, as the board are all responsible to the shareholders. If a director fails, it is usually because their reporting function has failed to deliver. Much will depend on how the fellow directors feel about the efforts and direction involved as to whether it is the individual with the functional responsibility who must pay any penalty for the failure. Team responsibility tends to remain with the manager, but whichever way you view it, responsibility only really becomes an issue when the team fails. If it succeeds it should be accepted that it was a team effort, although outsiders may well give undue credit to good management.

A manager whose authority is only respected when backed up by disciplinary sanctions, has little authority to affect the team in other than a negative way. Peer group pressure is a far stronger enforcer of discipline in the long term than any penalty imposed from a position of authority, even if the manager is free to adopt a hire and fire approach. In fact, if the team consider the penalty unjustified, the leader will have taken a major step towards creating a 'him and us' situation. The exercise of formal authority as a leader is only indicated when the team is in unresolvable conflict within itself and probably already on a course towards failure.

Create a complete team; operate as a team built of equals; work at developing as a team; resolve conflict early through discussion and counselling and support each other and these issues should never arise. Success means that management authority and responsibility remain only theoretical issues.

MATRIX WORKING

The times when authority and responsibility do get drawn into the spotlight are when team members are expected to work successfully in a number of teams, as a result of the organisation adopting a matrix work structure for assembling a team across several functional areas.

In many cases the issue arises because the methods have been used to create and run a specially created team, to implement total quality management, for example. The experience of working in a new team, where the tasks assigned are those you prefer to do, can often result in those parts of the job which are a poor fit in the original team starting to slip. Naturally the manager concerned will wish to ensure that his team is successful, yet our dual team member may well respond with meeting the demands of *both* teams – some slippage is inevitable.

The next stage is that the line manager reaches the point where he may invoke his authority in an attempt to enforce compliance in the completion of these out of role tasks – trying to get an Enabler to complete a detailed report for example. If the task still gets overlooked or is dashed off to get it out of the way, the situation can deteriorate to a full confrontation. Emotive subjects like 'loyalty' and 'lack of effort' begin to enter the conversation.

Our team member, used to openness and discussion in his new team, may well respond to his manager, who has not been exposed to role based team working concepts, with a burst of incomprehensible jargon, which appears to question his leadership style and by implication, his ability as a leader. It may even get to the point where the subordinate says: 'I'm a Driver/Enabler, not a Controller, if you wanted that job done so badly, you should have given it to X.' From here it is a small step to 'Who do you think is running this team?' and the rejoinder: 'If you would only let this team run itself, it would all work a lot better.'

To prevent this clash of team cultures from arising, it must be accepted that in an organisation which intends to apply matrix working, introducing the concepts of a team built of equals to a team which has to operate across the lines of function management, without exposing those managers who will have to work with these team members to the same concepts and experiences, is a recipe for conflict.

Far better, especially if you wish to test the approach before wider implementation in the organisation, is to pick a team with a tightly defined job to do within the line management structure. Look on it as containing the infection if you like, for the enthusiasm and interest generated by a successful team working as a team built of equals can be highly contagious!

9

Under Performing Teams

Whenever an organisation looks at its team working, there are always teams that under perform. Most teams respond well to the methods outlined in the earlier chapters, but there may be some teams where circumstances may well prevent a fully satisfactory implementation. In others, after an initial burst of enthusiasm, they fail to develop as expected.

The solutions proposed for all but the last of these problem teams are strictly in the category of what to do when all else fails within an acceptable time frame. Spotting the true causes of the team's problems may prove easy, as in the case of our first problem team which must learn to operate shorthanded, or require a more subtle analysis as in the case of the Politician's team.

- The Shorthanded Team.
- The Team of Individualists.
- The Lightweight Team.
- The Politician's Team.
- The One Man Band.

THE SHORTHANDED TEAM

Symptoms: a high level of effort and commitment still result in this team missing deadlines and drifting over cost budget. Tasks which everyone agrees should be done still don't get done because other tasks intervene. A typical team in trouble.

The shorthanded team is by definition one without a full set of roles and *at the same time* one constrained by circumstances from fixing that element of their problems. There will always be some cases where there is no opportunity at all to balance the team. A typical example is the team of Drivers so often found at the start of a business venture.

They are all Drivers, as their primary role preference. It's usually one of the reasons why they have become entrepreneurs, but it's doubtful that team structure was high on their list of priorities at the time they started their venture. Their team will therefore be dynamic but fragile, as the early history of entrepreneurial ventures often shows.

The first step for a shorthanded team of this nature is to recognise that they are indeed all Drivers. As this team cannot change, being totally constrained by the knowledge, skills and financial blend of personnel that is the foundation of their company, recognising they are all Drivers will at least identify their strengths and may also impose a degree of untypical, but necessary caution upon them. As the next step, they must look at the mix of secondary role preferences and at least try to allocate tasks accordingly. It is regrettably the case in teams of this nature that this will not take them much further on, as they are typically missing more than one role, even after the role transfer stage. Finally, they must find out what characteristics are totally missing from the team and take a good hard look at the task areas which are being ignored. This will show where the underlying weakness of their missing roles is most likely to lead to crises or even failure. The short term planning and lack of control data which stems from having no Planner and Controller, may not bring our entrepreneurial team down immediately, but the cumulative effects can become extremely damaging and expensive.

To a team which does not know about roles and why tasks get put off until a crisis has been provoked, operating with one or two missing roles is often the most insidious danger, because it's hard to recognise. Time and again the same tasks do not get done for all sorts of apparently valid reasons, but because they do not get done, the deadline keeps being moved backwards. Often, this is the first clue.

Deciding that you will get back on track if everybody works harder is *not* the right answer. Everybody will simply work harder at the jobs they instinctively like and know they do well, and that was not the problem in the first place. When good work is being done by all around you, yet progress towards the objective is inching along when it should be racing, you have probably found a missing role bottleneck.

The team is effectively shorthanded. Not in numbers: some may even have no work to do and seem to stand around as others on the team ply their skills and stretch their abilities to the limit. It's not going to get much easier from here on, but at least this will become a conscious battle to complete those tasks that all on the team know that none of them really wish to take on and will continue to put off without considerable support and self-discipline.

So how should you decide who should take on the Planning tasks when there is no Planner on the team? Start by pinning down exactly which tasks are not getting done. Have they been assigned to someone already, or have they been ignored totally? First look at the tasks everyone agreed should be done. Don't shout too loudly at whosoever was assigned to do them. Assuming they are neither lazy nor idiots, it was the team's fault for assigning them blindly.

Then reassign the tasks. Not on the basis of whose area of knowledge it may be, (such as getting the computer organised and installed, therefore assigning it to the computer programmer) but on what kind of task it is. In this case getting a specified resource when and where it is needed. So if it involves getting resources, reassign it to whoever displays a preference for the Enabler as their secondary role, even if all they know about computers could be written on the back of a postage stamp. They will treat the gaining of enough information to identify the best deal as just another resource to be found.

If no one has the slightest desire to take on the role of Enabler, then at least you know what the problem is. If they cannot face the complete role, is there anybody who scores more than 10 for the Resource Manager characteristic to have a shot at it? If the answer is still no, try and split it between two people who scored 8 each as Resource Managers; at least that should be better than leaving it with the computer person, particularly if they scored 5 or less for the characteristic.

If all else fails, take the missing role and allocate its tasks among the members, accepting that both the Monitor and Co-ordinator are going to have to work overtime. The rest of the team have not solved the problem just by assigning it, but will need to allow time to input to these tasks when requested. The one line assignments in the role sections which follow are designed to dovetail with the role preferences of the nominated roles, but are not complete substitutions. The advice which follows must be considered as a last resort, if you really cannot change the constitution of the team. It will always be better to recruit or co-opt if you can.

When assigning the tasks for each role, accept that certain tasks will require whole team input and pass out the rest as follows:

Driver

- The Enabler to ensure that the team seeks and recognises new opportunities for growth.

- The Exec and Enabler to keep the team ready to grasp the opportunities offered.

- The Controller to make sure changes actually occur, fast enough to be of some use.

The whole team will have to attempt to problem solve and make decisions. Meet as a team and get the Exec and Controller to identify the problems and decisions to be made on the day. Make a list and resist all attempts to defer taking the decisions or solving the problems. Any item appearing more than twice on such a list must either be dealt with at once or else someone must be co-opted temporarily to act for the team in the matter. It may well help to take an arbitrary decision, then poll the team for their first reaction, having made it. Feel free to change it *once only*. For a team without a Driver, no decision is a bad decision.

Planner

- The Controller to identify and gather the facts needed to define the team's goals and strategy.

- The Enabler and Controller to persuade people from other areas to join in the team's planning.

- The Controller to check that it is technically, operationally and financially feasible for the team to pursue a given course of action.

The whole team will have to input to the scheduling process, bearing in mind the Driver's preference for setting short deadlines and the Exec's for plenty of time in which to get the work done. The best you can hope for is that the Controller may have some data on how long a similar task took in the past.

Get out the diaries, set at least four firm dates and plan time for working together to refine those areas where the team's experience and specialised knowledge can be harnessed to input to the planning process. The first session will tell you what you don't know; use the second to draft the strategies; the third to work on feasibility and costings; the last to draw up a progress control calendar for the next three periods be they weeks, months or years. Repeat the last meeting at appropriate intervals, always before reaching the end of the third plan period.

Enabler

■ The Controller to ensure that problems in getting resources for the team are identified and overcome.

■ The Planner to determine the sort of team wanted and the profiles of the members needed to create it.

■ The Driver to represent the team to the rest of the organisation and to raise the team's bargaining status.

The whole team will have to work at motivation and communication. The Driver must never assume that the team shares a vision of the future and should take the time to expound the benefits that will accrue to all; the Planner should remind the team of where they are going; the Exec of the achievements of the day and the Controller of how much real progress has been made. The whole team should take the time to let others know what they are trying to do and have achieved.

Exec

■ The Controller to analyse the instructions the team receives and clarify them for everyone to understand.

■ The Enabler to communicate and handle any conflicting demands made on the team.

■ The Planner to set the day to day targets which keep the team productive and on track.

The whole team will have to watch out for and support each other, especially when personal problems or pressure lead to symptoms of stress. The Enabler will have to hone listening skills; the Controller those of observation; the Planner look ahead for likely points of pressure and the Driver learn patience and take the time to hear the full story before proposing a solution.

Controller

■ The Exec finds how best to set up a way to monitor the team's progress and keep track of problems.

- The Enabler to check the quality of the team's resources.
- The Planner to check the quality of the team's systems.

The whole team will need to look at whether all their combined efforts have achieved their original aims and give value for the effort invested. The Driver will need to guard against changing course too often, while the Enabler must restrain the inclination to propose a diversion off the track when the going, towards the planned future, gets tough. The Exec must lift their head from the work occasionally and look around, while the Planner take time to look at the past as well as the future. All involved must look outwards to see what effect the team's work is having on those with whom they interact and those who form the team's client group.

The shorthanded team always leaves some area of the work undone until there is a crisis to focus their attention, but at least the gaps are predictable. Harder to work with and develop is the team which has no real desire to be a team.

THE TEAM OF INDIVIDUALISTS

Symptoms: Few meetings and some of the team end up missing even these. Members accept complete projects from the team and attempt them without question. Little or no working together.

Individualists are more common than you might think, given that most people think teams are a good thing and should be encouraged. Our definition of an individualist is somewhat specialised: we don't mean non- conformist or eccentric (although they may also demonstrate these tendencies) but only a person who does not naturally welcome teamwork.

There are many jobs and careers which place a premium in performance terms on working alone or on one's own initiative. Some are obvious, such as salesmen or business consultants, others less so such as teachers, writers and computer programmers. Some may turn out to be true loners because the jobs they have always done are inherently 'one-person' in nature, such as art, design, photography and research. They prove hard to handle within a team, but their skills are often extremely valuable.

If they have had a bad experience with team working in the past – (as we saw in Chapter 5) in badly assembled and often unsuccessful teams, which were really committees in all but name

– it may be possible to show them that things need not always be that bad. Start by taking them through the team development process outlined in earlier chapters. They may well then express a willingness to give teamwork one more try. Be extra watchful: at the first sign of a setback, they may well return to a hidden agenda on which team activities have a low priority.

If such individualists are mature enough and can be persuaded to accept teamwork as valid for this particular job – to put their individualism into suspended animation, at least temporarily – all may work out fine with a bit of extra effort by the team's Exec on co-ordination. If they are not (and many talented people aren't) then don't include them in the team but, instead, regard them as any specialist resource you may need to call on and let your Enabler handle them.

It is very rare to find a team made up entirely of those who admit to being individualists, but even if they say they prefer team working, you will find that many people have been conditioned by the jobs listed above, only to work as individuals. If individualists are in the majority the chances of the team attaining a significant level of cohesion are much reduced. This is especially so if the task requires a high level of independent operation which reinforces the feeling of separateness, such as an export drive by the organisation.

A team of individualists may come together with as much early enthusiasm for a new challenge as any other team. The reason that this team often under performs, even if all the roles are present, is because they gradually become indifferent to the needs of the team as their own priorities return to prominence.

There is only one known cure: a heavy dose of co-ordination by the Exec on the team. Indeed if you can find two or even three Execs to work in the team, they can elicit a level of performance from these independent talents which is highly productive. If the team's independent operators feel that there is someone prepared to listen and act in support, they may come to depend on the day to day contact and be drawn closer into the team. The keynote is a regular and maintained level of communication as a counter to the development of indifference to the aims of the team and the return of the individualist's personal agenda as the primary motivator.

THE LIGHTWEIGHT TEAM

Symptoms: They work fairly well together, have a full complement of roles, but somehow always disappoint. There may be no technical reasons why they should not perform as other teams do, but they just seem contented to jog along.

There will always be differences in performance between seemingly identical teams, even those engaged in similar tasks. It must never be forgotten, in the first flush of enthusiasm which follows the identification of the team's preferred roles, the reassignment of the tasks to create a better team fit and the planning for team development, that the world is populated by people with varying degrees of knowledge and capabilities, capacity for hard work, levels of ambition and life goals.

The list of personal attributes could go on and on, some enhancing, others weakening the team. All you can hope to do by working as a team of equals is to produce the best performance of which that team is capable. If that is still not good enough, you have the roles to identify and fix the problem – the combination of the Controller to identify the real causes and the Enabler to provide the training resource provides the best way forward.

That is fine if you have the time and the will to fix it, but often the root of the trouble with a lightweight team is that their expectations are too low. They really don't believe they have a problem – after all things always take longer than the plan said that they should, don't they? In serious cases this can be exacerbated by some of the members adopting a 'George will do it' mentality. They know that if they leave it long enough and keep thinking up excuses some other more co-operative team member, or their frustrated team leader, will do it for them.

Assuming that the team has not been given a task way beyond their capabilities, which no amount of team development will resolve, what can you do to extract the level of performance you require? There is no single answer. Take the time to counsel each team member to see if you can identify a personal problem which is reducing performance, and, if you then draw a blank, you could then safely try any of the following tactics:

- A transfusion of new blood. As long as the team has a complete set of roles, review with the team's Controller which tasks appear to be causing the most loss of performance. Then look for an active candidate with a role combination that will offer the greatest benefit from role sharing.

- A team planning review. Emphasise the need to revise schedules to try and win back some of the lost time. Go for dated commitments from each team member for completion of the agreed tasks.

- A report, prepared by the Controller, of the team's performance with a comparative analysis with the second best team in the organisation. Then get the team to use this information to plan their own performance improvement.

- Increase the frequency but drastically shorten the length of team meetings. Try a series of meetings with only single role agendas.

- Second each of the team's members in rotation on an exchange basis with more successful teams. (This is the easiest way to determine if all that this team is suffering from is one rotten apple spoiling the barrel.)

THE POLITICIAN'S TEAM

Symptoms: This team meets often and maintains a high profile, yet produces little except reports. It also works apart just like a team of individualists, with one critical exception: they will all tell you that they are totally committed to team working.

This team talks like a brilliant team. Their meetings are often inspiring, well chaired, run to time and they produce immaculate minutes. The only trouble is they don't actually get a lot done. A look at their diaries soon tells you why: they don't actually have time between meetings to get much done except prepare for their next meeting.

In reality, all these players are good committee types rather than teamworkers. The team, in their terms, only exists to hold meetings. From their viewpoint the organisation only exists to promote their status and further their careers, so be on your guard! New initiatives with wide ranging impact, such as constructing a team built of equals, are often the subject of attempted hijacks by such a team, who see the process of change as a way to climb one more rung up the ladder.

Hopefully, in team terms, this is becoming a dying breed, but it still tends to proliferate in the 'good times' in medium to large corporate environments as self diagnosed high flyers or ambitious trade unionists spent their time playing political games in an attempt to make it to the top. The civil service and local government are also breeding grounds for this type of team. Recession has put the squeeze on them, the compression of organisational hierarchies has given them fewer opportunities to manoeuvre, but you may find a residue of the type appearing in senior teams – many of these players are great survivors.

To spot an individual player look for the signs of the Driver Reinforcement syndrome described in Chapter 5. Their political skills and networking abilities often result in them gaining appointment as team leaders. The danger only becomes acute when other players in the same mould succeed in joining the team. As the primary motivation for this group is to increase power and influence, the team may end up growing quite rapidly as it is promulgated that their lack of progress is due to a lack of personnel to cover vital areas. In no time at all the team may achieve BigTeam status, having reached double figures in numbers, but still will not produce more than a straightforward and productive team half their size.

If it's all that obvious, why does it succeed in furthering the ambitions of the players (rather than the teamworkers) involved? The answer is that they are often talented people whose orientation is entirely towards their own personal goals. Those around them who are trying to get a job done, are looking at the tasks. They may grumble about the politician, but they rarely get to the point of being able to do anything about it, unless the long knives come out towards the end of a project when it is already too late. These are people who spend much of their creative energies looking for ways to move onwards and upwards, which, let's face it, can be a lot of fun if you enjoy playing that sort of game!

Little can be done about the Politician's team from the bottom up. The solution (if any) has to come from the top down, preferably from someone clearly seen to be in a position of greater power – even then it can prove dangerous to your organisational health! These people will not stop trying and will use every political trick to resist diversion from their aims. The soundest approach is to limit the number of teams they are allowed to join, then insist on detailed planning and enlist a dedicated Controller into the team. They will never be really productive in a team environment until they learn to appreciate the satisfaction to be gained from being part of a successful team more than the personal gratification of scrambling up the career ladder.

THE ONE MAN BAND

Symptoms: Only one person seems to know what is really going on and their version is often at odds with that of the rest of the team. Time is wasted by one member redoing work done by others. Some of the team are under utilised.

A common problem team, especially when a young manager is first put in charge. It primarily occurs when someone attempts to impose their vision on the team down to the smallest point of detail. The conventional solution is to provide training in delegation, but that assumes that, what will be eventually delivered, matches exactly the expectations of the delegator: often they will reject real improvements because they were not part of the original vision.

Look for the Driver/Exec role combination – the 'First I decide what we are going to do and then I do it' scenario. Other signs are an almost pathetic eagerness to succeed, coupled in many cases with a naïvety of the final delivery, as the team's experience and skills have not been utilised.

The solution is the simplest one of all: a period of coaching to help this team develop fully as a team of equals. This team is suffering from a case of arrested development. Not letting go is usually a sign of insecurity. The clear understanding of the tasks to be done to be successful, the supportive nature of the approach and the understanding of how and where everyone can best contribute will count for nothing if someone on the team simply cannot let go. After they show signs of confidence and are beginning to work as a team, take care not to just walk away and leave them to get on with it, but continue the treatment by coaching and counselling at regular intervals as the work progresses, otherwise the first reversal may cause them to suffer a relapse.

10

What You Can Achieve

By this chapter you will probably know your own role preferences quite well and have begun to think about applying the methodology outlined in this book to a team. There may still be some doubts in your mind as to whether this team will benefit and just what you can expect to achieve.

TEAMS THAT WILL BENEFIT

We find at this stage that the question people most want answered is: 'What sort of team have I got (or do I need)?, 'Is it a real team?'

The definition of a real team is a group of less than ten people, who need to combine and work together to achieve a common goal *and produce a result which can be seen to be greater than the same number of people working entirely separately.* Few teams achieve this ideal on a regular basis, but don't let that put you off! Think about your team: do you think they could be a real team? You may be able to answer 'yes' with certainty; 'no', but perhaps that is because you have some reservations, or you may feel that you need more information to decide.

Yes: If the answer is yes, the need for a composite team with a full set of roles is obvious. The only decisions relate to how to achieve it. To help you plan, we have provided an action plan checklist in the section entitled 'What are you going to do now?' at the end of this chapter.

No: If the answer is no, you must first decide if your definition of your team is too limited and you should be trying to identify the full team that you need to be successful. A sales team which requires a sales office, technical support and marketing back-up to operate successfully, should not exclude representatives from all these areas from their team. A surgical team may need to include those who will carry out the post operative care, and involve a Planner/Co-ordinator to ensure that operating theatre resources are fully utilised.

In the case of a specialist group – if there are individuals who need to come together on occasion as a real team from within the larger group – the time to identify them is now, rather than when a crisis forces them all to try to learn how to work together. To create a real team of this nature, set them the goal of improving the whole group's performance in some area: quality, productivity, and forward planning are possible starting points.

Once you have this first group in place, what about the others? Have they nothing to contribute? They may certainly feel excluded if the first team begins to gel. There are two courses of action open to you at this point. The first is essential if you don't wish to be accused of ignoring the rest of the group, the second is optional, but will certainly pay off in the longer term:

1. Make sure you get your Planner to seek input to the team's plans from the wider group. Follow this up by getting your team's Enablers to take the time to let all around them in the wider group know both your intentions and what is happening on a regular basis. Don't wait until your team appears with its new minted ideas before telling those they affect all about them. Consultation, participation and antic-ipation can work for you to get your ideas accepted and used. Ignore this, and the inertia and resistance from the wider group may dissipate the team's efforts to the point of oblivion.

2. Assemble a second team or even a series of teams and get them working towards a suitable goal. It may help to place a member from your first group team in each of these additional teams. If they are used to working as a team of equals, they will be able to guide the others to get started successfully. As time goes by and people move on, you will also have a most valuable resource to call upon: a group of people to recruit from to join the core team, who are already practised team workers.

More information required: To help you, here is a list of the types of teams that we have seen benefit:

-   Company Boards – from three to eight members.

- Management Teams – in both the public and private sectors, including education, health care, local government, national and multi-national companies.

- Project Teams – construction, new product development, contract management, process development and manufacturing.

- Professional Teams – lawyers, accountants, management consultants, advertising agencies, marketing.

- Business Development Teams – home markets and exports, for both manufacturing and service industries.

- Specialist teams – research and development, production, sales and marketing, technical service, quality control.

Add to this list teams brought together to manage company moves, acquisition and divestment programmes, disaster and crisis response teams, teams involved in the management of technical or cultural change.

If you cannot see your team here, don't feel disheartened. Providing you can decide on a goal to work towards and have a group small enough to interact and work together as a unit, you can succeed in creating a team of equals.

To achieve this implies a readiness to change on your part and on the part of the team. The most fundamental changes required of someone who has gone through a traditional management training are to learn to pass the leader's baton to promote contribution in task areas unrelated to your preferred role; to resist the temptation to communicate in managerial vein and tell your group what you want done and how to do it. The motivation for this change must be based on the desire to try and gain more satisfaction from generating a full contribution from everyone in the team rather than from imposing your will upon the rest of the team. Do not forget they will be expecting you to make a full contribution in your turn – this is not a recipe for sitting back and prodding the rest of them to do all the work.

As far as the team is concerned, to succeed in this means that all the parties concerned will have to be prepared to change the way they look at each other: to step out from behind the function labels (engineer, salesman, accountant) they have worn as a badge of office up to now. The identification of the roles each person prefers to play in a team is the first step in the process. The next step may prove quite hard: it means abandoning the 'not my job' thinking when working as part of the team and making a full contribution in those tasks that require input from your role.

Until you have tried it, you will have to take our word for it that it's worth the effort. Once you have tried it, team working becomes one of the pleasures of life, instead of what too many people find it: a way of working which requires them to suppress personal inclination 'for the good of the team'.

PERSONAL DEVELOPMENT

On completion of the role preference questionnaire and reading the description and advice which relate to your role, there is always the temptation to turn aside from the issues of team working and consider the implication for one's own career development. One word of caution: all that we are measuring in this book are your preferences in terms of the tasks you prefer to take on in a team situation. While this has relevance in clarifying in one's mind the types of task we can approach with some confidence, this was never designed to serve as a basis for future career planning. For this purpose, role preference seems to work best at showing you what type of work you should try and avoid!

That is not to say that we have never known people whose careers have been transformed by taking part in a teambuilding exercise. The impact tends to affect people in one or all of the following ways:

1. *They discover that behaviour which they have been suppressing, as they believed it to be unacceptable in the organisation's culture, is not only acceptable but valued.* A typical case was that of a school teacher who had restrained his Driver role preference and contributed little to problem solving and decision making, as he did not feel he could impose his ideas on the team. As a result he was regarded as a stick in the mud, who just agreed with what the majority wanted and had no real views of his own. Once he discovered that the team welcomed his role, he felt free to step forward. His confidence rose; he felt valued for his ideas. After 20 years in the profession, he restarted his career, became a Deputy Head and then was successful in gaining a position as a Headmaster within three years.

2. *They learn how to work with other people.* So many of us either end up working for someone or have people working for us.

How many times can you honestly say you have worked effectively *with* a whole team? Partnerships of two people are quite common and there are those whose advice on team assembly says that you should never separate a productive partnership, although in our experience you will often find that they share the same role. Knowing what tasks each member of the team prefers to do is the key to being able to ask them to work with you. Pick those parts of your job where, although you may have the specialised knowledge required, you know in your heart of hearts that you need someone to help you with some aspect of the wider task, such as presentation or planning. Learn to like sharing the work with others and to accept their contribution, (not forgetting to help them in return) and you will not only be more effective, but you will build a network of contacts which will serve you well in the future.

3. *They learn how to generate a contribution at any level in the organisation.* Adopting and developing the Moderator leadership style can increase not only your effectiveness but your popularity. You remain in control, but not through the process of issuing orders. You make fewer mistakes as you gain input to solutions from several sources. You are seen to listen and seek consensus whenever possible.

The last point to consider on personal development is your future training plan. Now that you can see where you prefer to contribute in any team, make sure that the training you select enhances those areas of contribution and resist the temptation to try and become all things to all men. The objective should be to develop those skills and techniques related to those essential differences, which make you more effective and thus of greater value in your role. The alternative is to try to become a clone of some mythical all-rounder, the 'jack-of-all-trades' who is master of none. It is the diversity of contribution which makes a good team such a stimulating place to work, not the homogeneity of conforming to a single pattern, however 'rounded' it may be.

HOME USE – IS THERE A FAMILY TEAM?

The problem with creating programmes and books which are based on questionnaires and then give advice is that, as any magazine publisher will tell you, everyone likes to do a question-naire. If the results prove to be accurate – and with a questionnaire that has been tested and used as many times as this one, this tends to be the case – people often try to extend a carefully designed psychological tool into areas for which it was not designed.

It may sound on a par with advice from an agony aunt to talk about the family team, but provided that you don't try to read too much into it in this out of context situation, you may find some useful pointers for coping with family life, particularly in relating to the emphasis the other half of the team may put on certain activities.

The point to remember is that no one in a family group can be seen simply as whatever it may say on the role label and that in any case we are only looking at your preferences for working in a real team. Then, also, most people have a secondary role preference that will introduce a degree of flexibility and that can provide the element of lubricant that makes it all run smoother. If the family is under pressure, you must never forget that people make role and communication shifts which will revert when the pressure is reduced.

So, with these provisos, by all means enjoy yourselves and have a go at the questionnaire, it may let you see those around you in a new light and even be a bit more tolerant when they don't do things your way!

HARMONY, BALANCE AND PRODUCTIVITY

This ability to take a fresh look at those around in your team through understanding of role preference and the effects that role can have on the team, is central to the way a team built of equals can lead to the creation of a team which works in harmony, strikes a healthy balance and achieves productivity.

In the early stages, harmony may well seem to be the last thing this approach is likely to generate. If you have been sitting comfortably in a homogeneous team, a cozy group of like minds, completing the team may spark conflicts as role opposites clash for the first time. As one team member from a formerly Driver/Enabler based team put it to us about the team's new Controller: 'I know why he's there, but you have to learn to bite your tongue'.

If you are a fast-track role type it is no use letting rip your frustration when a Planner insists on going into detail and warning of the potential risks. That is what they are there for. If you ignore their contributions, you may end up like so many organisations led by a Driver or Enabler, who run into trouble through a combination of too much speed and too little planning and feedback. Let it go too far and they can find themselves with a Controller appointed from outside to lead the team (usually from a financial discipline) to calm them down and bring them to heel. Of course, as we have seen from the Controller's team case study, too much of this role can be just as damaging.

Only by putting a real team on it can true balance be achieved. *Successful Team Building* shows you where to look to achieve this balance, but only by working at it, will it become reality. Take a tip from one formerly explosive Managing Director: whenever he was tempted to let go or felt that the frustrations of listening to negative analysis from the team's Financial Controller were about to trigger a heart attack, he took his doctor's advice, drew a deep breath and exhaled slowly counting to ten. It seemed to work. More and more he observed that if you gave the accountant time, he usually had a valid point to make, after the somewhat protracted analysis. This started him thinking and he began to apply the same approach to the other roles on the team as well. Formerly the first to jump in, thus usually stopping the discussion stone dead, he began consciously to attempt to make his contributions among the last on any subject. To try and ensure that he was not butting in too soon, he encouraged all around him to have their say first, even when requested for his views.

As a result of the doctor's advice, the Managing Director's leadership style, formerly so brusque, fast-track and positive, had moved towards that of a Moderator, but he still felt that it was not a natural way to act. He certainly was no less positive and seemed to be more effective: promoting team harmony by requesting input from others before making his own contribution (which he had time to reflect on and modify as the meetings progressed) and ultimately his team was more productive as everyone felt that their ideas had received an airing and that they had been fully involved in the decision making process. All this resulted in the team accepting full ownership of the plans and objectives.

Once this team had discovered their role preferences and begun to attempt to use the Moderator style for themselves, much of the pressure to restrain his natural role was lifted from the Managing Director, who in role terms had been projecting the style of a Planner in order to achieve the level of input he felt essential. It also reduced an element of bias caused by this less natural approach, as the Managing Director was largely suppressing the positive aspects of the Driver role along with the negative fast track effects.

Adopting only one aspect of the approach, the Moderator like style was not sufficient. The team only achieved balance once they had gained an understanding of roles and their effects and learned to work with the full programme.

These changes may seem too small to achieve more than marginal improvements in productivity, until you take a closer look at where the gains are to be made:

- Jobs run to time. This does not necessarily mean quicker, but should allow optimum use of resources. In addition, it may offer scope for savings in the additional expenses incurred if things run late: rush fees, overtime, purchasing more expensive substitutes for the sake of speed.

- Jobs get done right, *once!* Quality improves, re-work declines.

- Stress is reduced. Instead of being drained by adrenalin fatigue, people are fresher and produce more as a result.

- The team works together. Not just throwing bodies at their problems, but in a structured way which allows the right combination of people to work on each task, getting it done quicker and more effectively.

- Tasks don't get put off. No more 'ignore it and it will go away' thinking, or 'leave it in the in tray and if they haven't asked for it in a fortnight, bin it' working. How many times have you started and stopped a task you disliked, wasting time and effort before you finished it? This can impact on the entire team's productivity, particularly if you are stuck in the middle of the team's missing role.

The cost of a low productivity team can be far more than their salary and associated payroll costs, which for a team of five senior members can easily exceed £1,000 an hour, but may also impact in lost orders; increased production costs; extended waiting lists or delivery times; eroded market share; wasted publicity costs; poor machine utilisation and the costs of additional resources that are necessary to achieve the original goal. Often the choice is between coming in on time or on budget – yet missing either of these targets can prove extremely damaging to an organisation.

CULTURE

If we were to pick one phrase to encapsulate the culture of a team built of equals, it is simply this: Don't waste people.

It's not just that for most companies they are the largest element of cost. Nor that the unproductive are a drain on the national resources. It's far simpler than that. Every time you assign a task to someone which they put off doing, you will end up wasting hours of people's lives – your own included! Every time a team or just an individual fails, they will have wasted much of that time. If as a result of this failure, the knock on effects make people redundant or simply prevent progress and improvement, more people will be wasted. Eliminate this waste wherever and whenever you can and you not only improve your organisation's efficiency and effectiveness, but actually enrich the lives of others.

As one of our team is fond of saying: 'If it's not fun, don't do it!' When asked 'Why not?' the response is always: 'We pass this way but once.' If you are working in teams where every task is a chore, there is never enough time to cope with all the demands on your time and the final result always gets hacked to pieces in committee and has to be redone, it's only a masochist who will find any element of fun. Of course the Puritan streak which still emerges from time to time may say 'Well, what did you expect? It's work!'.

Our view of work is that it should be as satisfying and enjoyable as possible. Starting by assigning all concerned in a team the tasks they prefer to do seems a good place to start and as far as we are concerned it is only the start. Human companionship, working *with* each other; sharing and supporting; recognising the value of work done by others and receiving recognition in your turn; being able to say at the end of the day 'That went well' and to look forward to the next day, making a real contribution and encouraging others to do the same. Surely all teamwork should be like that? If, between you, you can create a team of equals you will achieve it.

The wider cultural impact we have discussed in earlier chapters. Suffice it to say here that we believe that the team built of equals is completely in tune with and supportive of the cultural aspirations of a work force for the nineties.

Team and company health checks

Assuming that you would like to attempt to reap the benefits and satisfaction from working in a team of equals and arrive bright-eyed and bushy tailed on a Monday morning ready to change the world for the better; you may find that there are those around you who will need to be convinced that there is anything wrong.

The quickest way to show them that the symptoms of poor team working are real and that stress is the unfortunate result, is to try this simple ten question health check. This has been stripped down to bare essentials so that it will work for a team or a company equally well. Ask the questions and note down the number of times you get agreement acknowledging a symptom.

1. People are often late or even 'have to' miss meetings.

2. Positions are entrenched by job function ('it's not my job').

3. Too much time is spent going over the same old ground.

4. Jobs are assigned to individuals which are almost complete projects in their own right.

5. Too much work is changed or has to be redone after a team meeting.

6. One or more people at any team meeting seems to have their own hidden agenda.

7. People accept tasks for a team, but never seem to get them done on time.

8. Deadlines are set just far enough away that you can't really argue with them, but there are too few detailed plans.

9. Teams seem to produce long reports but are short on real output.

10. Priorities keep being changed as problems arise.

If you get agreement to more than three of these statements you will certainly benefit. Five or more and you have a serious problem with the likelihood of some people being at risk from stress. Turn to the next section and start your action plan now!

WHAT ARE YOU GOING TO DO NOW?

Assuming that by this stage you have reached the point of wishing to apply what you have learned, where is the best place to start?

The first step is to bring everyone else affected by your initiative up to speed. Getting them to do the questionnaire and read this book is the easiest way of doing it. When you look at the full costs of running a team, you can see why major companies pay several thousand pounds to run our TEAMBuilder programme, so why not start by buying everyone their own copy of *Successful Team Building*? Then you can make full use of the checklist steps below.

1. Get everyone to complete their role analysis.

2. Review their results and discuss with them:
   a) Role shifts.
   b) Communication style.
   c) Team experience – how do they rate themselves?
   d) Which areas of the role do they think would benefit from task oriented training?

3. Draw up your team profile – have you a missing role?

3a. If yes, should you transfer, spread or recruit/co-opt?

4. Plan the first team meeting. Be sure to allow enough time for everyone to have a go at moderating the meeting.

5. At the first meeting, get each team member to commit to:
   a) looking again at their role and characteristic advice to select one new task to attempt for the team;
   b) identify a role based training need and inform the Enabler;
   c) working together with another team member on an appropriate task.

6. At the next meeting, concentrate on the Driver and Planner.
   a) Review and agree the team's goals and development objectives.
   b) Get the Planner to moderate the meeting to get input on strategy issues.
   c) Review task assignments and promote discussion of the missing role effects.
   d) Run a role based agenda for all the other team activities, making sure you get each role to moderate when it's their turn.

7. At the third meeting, concentrate on the Enabler and Exec.
   a) Get the Controller to issue a progress report to the Enabler before the meeting and start the meeting with a review of progress by the Enabler.
   b) Ask the Enabler to prepare an appropriate communication of the team's aims, objectives and progress for circulation outside the team.
   c) Talk over what has worked and what hasn't – get the Exec to moderate and review task assignments.

8. At the fourth meeting concentrate on the Driver and Controller.
   a) Ask the Controller to report on quality standards and how to measure them.
   b) Get everyone on the team in turn to raise problem areas.
   c) Get the Driver to moderate a problem solving session.

9. The fifth meeting, work through all the roles.
   a) Review resource issues – the Planner to highlight future needs, the Exec to highlight current shortfalls, the Enabler to sort out what to do to obtain them.
   b) Get the Driver's input on opportunities for the team.
   c) Ask the Controller for a progress report.
   d) Review training and take extra time to air views on role comfort as a topic. How is everyone coping? Have the changes gone far enough? Have things started to slip back?

You should, by now, be able see the patterns emerging. The successful team will take time to evolve. You will need to take stock at regular intervals and ventilate the team, making sure that everyone airs their views – you must never take silence to mean acquiescence.

Work at the techniques of moderating. Some teams find it useful to create the equivalent of a swear box – every time someone in the team forgets and issues an instruction before inviting contribution, they get to put a coin in the box – it's not only good for eradicating 'management-speak' from the team, some teams (particularly those with several Drivers!) have raised quite large sums for charity.

Above all try not to waste people. Get all the team to contribute. Make sure that individuals are given the opportunity to develop along with the team. Show that you recognise that they are different and that you value what they do and in time you will create your own successful team of equals.

EVERY ORG. PUB. OR PRIV SECT.
TRYES TO SELECT THE BEST TEAM
THROUGH THEIRS RECRUITM METHOL